Nobby 101
Have Boots, Do Travel. 102
Never Mind the Weather. 104
All Sorts of Hat-Tricks. 106
European Hot-Shots. 108
Go for the Double. 112
Phil Parkes Refused to Go to Scotland. 113
'Training' Funnies. 116
Near-Misses. 120
'Keeping Stars Fit' – by a top physiotherapist. 124

SHOOT! ANNUAL 1977

D0494995

£1.15

3

'My world-beating XI'

keep up with KEVIN KEEGAN

A favourite pastime of many players is to imagine themselves as managers and to pick teams. Sometimes it's basically adding one or two new faces to their own club or country team.

Often after being impressed with an outstanding player in an opposing team, or by someone in a televised match I'm watching, I've enjoyed pondering on how he would fit into the Liverpool or England side – or even both.

But I prefer selecting an entire team in my mind, and what really excites me is one made up of the men I consider to be supreme in their positions – a Kevin Keegan World eleven, in fact.

It's mind-boggling to contemplate managing a side with such a wealth of talent.

As my "number one," in goal, I have no hesitation in writing down the name of my club and country teammate, Ray Clemence. I know I'll be accused of favouritism

in some quarters, but I genuinely believe Ray is carrying on the English tradition of breeding the finest 'keepers on earth.

Ray, a worthy successor to Gordon Banks, has many qualities in common with Banksie – the right physique, bravery, and an uncanny positional sense that makes his job look so easy. Lesser 'keepers often appear much more spectacular, usually because they have been caught out in the wrong place and have been forced into making a desperate, fan-pleasing dive to pull off a save.

His handling is first-class, he never punches the ball when he can catch it, and is a master at cutting out dangerous crosses from the wings. Only rarely is he caught glued to his line.

No one is perfect, though, and his only fault is an occasional tendency to kick the ball into touch.

He's certainly come a long way from being a deck-chair attendant on the beach at Scunthorpe.

The World's best man-between-the-sticks is worthy of the finest back-four I can think of. For my left-back I select Enrique Woolf, whom many readers will remember from his memorable displays for Argentina in the 1974 World Cup in West Germany. One of the reasons he stood out is because he has something many experts regard as an advantage in this respect – blond hair.

Enrique is a specialist at one-two passes, revels in coming forward to join in attacks, and, most important of all, hardly ever gives the ball away.

On the opposite flank I'd place Paul Brietner, who is virtually a carbon copy of Enrique. He also is attack-minded, and besides being a goal-maker is well-qualified to take them, too. Remember the cracking drive from outside the penalty-area in West Germany's opening match against Chile which ended up in the back of the net?

Like several of the eye-catchers in that tournament he was snapped up shortly afterwards by a foreign club, moving from Bayern Munich to Real Madrid for £400,000.

No prizes for guessing my first choice as centre-back – Franz Beckenbauer, of course, dubbed "The Emperor" by his countless fans. There couldn't be a more apt title for a player who is majestic in everything he does.

CONTINUED ON PAGE 6

5

CONTINUED FROM PAGE 5

He above all others is mainly responsible for bringing the game's greatest honours to his club, Bayern Munich, and his country, West Germany. His coolness under pressure, such a steadying influence on his team-mates, never ceases to amaze me. For this one quality alone – and he possesses many more remarkable gifts – I appoint him my captain.

One of my dearest wishes is that I should have the privilege of playing under his captaincy. Unfortunately, it's likely to remain just a dream.

Wim Rijsbergen, the rock-steady Dutch international, completes my defence, to make a back-four to dishearten any striker. Wim is not only a good marker, an excellent passer of the ball, he is never embarrassed at being in possession and holds on to it until he can do something constructive.

If you're impressed with the potential of my defence, you'll be even more so with my three mid-fielders – Wlodimierez Deyna of Legia Warsaw and Poland, Johan Cruyff of Barcelona and Holland, and another West German international star, Berti Vogts of Borussia Munchengladbach.

Deyna isn't a fast-mover, hasn't a great shot, yet his other assets more than compensate for those deficiencies. He reads a game superbly, inspires those around him, and passes the "early" ball that gives the receiver valuable extra split-seconds in which to think before acting.

Perfection

He would provide a perfect foil for Johan Cruyff, the man who took over Pele's mantle as the greatest foot-baller in the World.

What can I say about Cruyff that hasn't already been said? He's just perfection in everything he does. Brain-power, ball-skill, fitness – you name it, Cruyff has it in full measure.

A scorer of incredible goals. After studying slow-motion replays of some of them, I've still been baffled as to how he's got the ball home.

In 1974, he moved from Dutch club Ajax to Barcelona in Spain.

Berti Vogts would be my ball-winner, the defensive-minded mid-fielder whose job is to rob the opposition and supply a service to team-mates.

I had first-hand experience of Berti's tigerish tackling and immaculate ball-distribution in Liverpool's two-legged U.E.F.A. Cup Final with Borussia in 1973. We won the Cup – even though the second-leg was in Borussia – but it was a close thing.

What I consider to be Berti's greatest feat was in stifling the menace of Johan Cruyff in an even more important Final – the World Cup Final between West Germany and Holland 1974.

I'd be hoping there would be no hard feelings lingering on between the two as a result.

Flair, the five-letter word that signifies so much in football – a combination of imagination, unique skill and remarkable character – is something every member of my team has, especially the forwards.

The first of my threesome is Ruben Ayala, the young Argentinian winger-cum-striker, with the dazzling turn of speed that stamps him as the fastest thing I've ever seen on a football pitch.

What also makes him distinctive is his long, flowing hair reminiscent of a footballing King Charles the First.

Now playing for Atletico Madrid, his technique of beating an opponent with the ball at full speed is one of the most thrilling sights in soccer.

For my second forward position I'd choose Uli Hoeness, a West German who came to the fore at an early age – joining the select handful of youngsters to win a World Cup medal. I'd play him on the opposite flank to Ayala.

A Challenge

And who is my "man in the middle" – the man to get most of the goals? I considered several big names until finally plumping for Andrzej Szarmach, the deadly Polish striker who finished joint second top-scorer in the 1974 World Cup competition with 5 goals.

Strictly a no-frills player, he certainly knows the whereabouts of the back of the net.

As my substitute, I'd pencil in Oleg Blochin, the player with Dynamo Kiev, which also doubles as the Russian team, who was voted European Player of the Year for 1975. Unfortunately I haven't seen enough of him to prefer him to one of my other selections.

So there you have it – my World team-: Clemence, Woolf, Brietner, Beckenbauer, Rijsbergen, Deyna, Cruyff, Vogts, Ayala, Hoeness and Szarmach. Sub: Blochin.

On the left Kevin, now an established England international, is shown in a typical attacking pose. He says that his club and country team-mate, Ray Clemence, shown below, is carrying on the English tradition of producing the finest 'keepers in the World, and unhesitatingly selects him as his "number one". On the right is the cool, calm and collected Franz Beckenbauer, the captain who has brought many honours to his club, Bayern Munich, and country, West Germany. One of Kevin's ambitions is to play alongside this extremely polished performer.

The fact I've included only one Briton – something that saddens me – is a reflection on the state of football in our Isles.

I'd play my team in an attacking 4–3–3 formation.

On paper the combination certainly looks more than a match for any permutation of top-class players from outside their ranks.

But would it be possible to blend such a mixture of rich talent? Would their temperaments clash?

It's an exciting challenge that I, as their manager, would accept like a shot!

Kevin Keegan

ES LEBE DIE SCHWEIZ ES LEBE ENGLAND SCHREIE FÜR BEIDE

LUCKY

ABOVE
England's Number One fan Ken Bailey has a message in German for Switzerland fans before a match.

RIGHT
Wolfgang Overath (left), captain of West German club I.FC Cologne, is presented with a pig(!) before the first game in Cologne's new stadium.

LEFT . . . Aldershot mascot Mark Wiseman watches Len Walker and Terry Paine of Hereford (right) shake hands.

RIGHT
Happy Celtic supporters wave mascots in the club's famous green-and-white colours before a game against Glasgow rivals Rangers.

MASCOTS

LEFT
The Tooting and Mitcham mascot was certainly lucky for the non-Leaguers in 1975/76, when they had a great F.A. Cup run.

BELOW
Berti Vogts, captain of West German aces Borussia Mönchengladbach, doesn't take much notice of the Wacker Innsbruck mascot as he runs out for a European Cup-tie.

JOE ROYLE
MANCHESTER CITY

10

Ipswich Town striker David Johnson looks smart around opponents' goal-mouths. He's always ready to snap up a half-chance.

The England international is smart off the field as well and most afternoons can be seen helping in his Ipswich boutique.

Football is a short career compared with most jobs and David is, no doubt, preparing for the day he must hang up his boots.

When our photographer called in on David at his shop, he found the Ipswich star and his boutique manager examining a new range of

What have Steve Heighway and Brian Hall (Liverpool), Alan Gowling (Newcastle), Peter Suddaby (Blackpool) and John Lacy (Fulham) in common? Answer: They all have University degrees.

Did you know that Hampden Park, "home" of Scottish international football, was named after an Englishman?

The Sassenach in question was John Hampden, the famous Roundhead M.P. at the time of the English Civil War.

He incurred the displeasure of King Charles I by trying to form a Scottish army to invade England.

In the closing years of the last century, a Glasgow builder, Mr. George Eadie—a great admirer of Hampden—called a row of villas he built on Prospecthill, Mount Florida, "Hampden Terrace" in honour of his hero.

It was next to the new ground being erected by the already-famous Queen's Park club and they decided to take the terrace's name for their stadium.

● Leo Callaghan, the former Football League referee, is happy with the laws of the game.

He said: "They do not need to be changed. The only problem is the professionalism at League level. If this could be cut out most of the problems would be solved."

As every soccer annual will tell you, the highest score ever achieved in Scottish football was Arbroath 36, Bon Accord 0.

But last season that record was broken by a LADIES soccer team . . . the Edinburgh Dynamos.

In an Eastern Region League Cup-tie the supergirls beat, or should I say annihilated, their opponents Lochend Thistle 42-0.

'MacDougall is tops'
says Arsenal's young defender DAVID O'LEARY

Just how good is Norwich City goal-king Ted MacDougall (main photo, right)?

Very good indeed, according to Arsenal defender David O'Leary (inset).

Says 18-year-old Dave, who established himself at Highbury last term: "I'd heard all sorts of reports about Ted before I actually played against him. Some people thought he could play a bit, but others weren't so keen.

"I found him a real handful. He is so quick he can be past you in a flash and he certainly knows the quickest route to goal.

"He's probably given me my hardest game to date.

"Even so, it was a real pleasure playing against him. He was very fair and quick to praise me when I did something right.

"I think Ted is a real gent."

● Southampton's midfield star Jim McCalliog holds something of a record among the hundreds of overseas clubs who have toured Australia.

Jim has played with three different clubs Down Under . . . Chelsea in 1963, Sheffield Wednesday in 1967 and Wolves in 1972.

● *Q.P.R. manager Dave Sexton is with his seventh London club after having played for West Ham and Crystal Palace and filled coaching and management posts with Chelsea, Orient, Fulham and Arsenal.*

But the late Ned Liddell was connected with eight.

He played for Orient and Arsenal, managed Q.P.R. and Fulham and was chief scout at West Ham, Chelsea, Brentford and Spurs.

What's soccer coming to? One Second Division manager whose club was caught in a relegation struggle last season, said "I think I'll employ a gypsy to bring us a change of luck."

We don't know if the man in question consulted a gypsy, but the club didn't go down.

ACE FULL-BACK

During a star-studded career with first Manchester City and now Burnley, Mike Summerbee has no doubts as to the best two full-backs he's ever faced.

"It is difficult to find genius at full-back," he says. "You normally associate star players with forwards. But for my money there were no better players than England's Ray Wilson and Terry Cooper.

"In any list of world class players they must be included. I have played against full-back Ray Wilson many times and don't remember ever beating him."

Recognise the keen gardener? He's Fulham's popular goalkeeper Peter Mellor. "It's a great way to keep fit," said Peter.

The Doc v. Sir Matt Busby

Manchester United's rise under Tommy Docherty must have prompted comparisons between him and former manager Sir Matt Busby, now a director, who helped bring so much success to the club during the Forties, Fifties, and Sixties.

What are the two men like?

Who better to answer that question than the present, longest-serving member on the playing staff at Old Trafford, 'keeper Alex Stepney.

"Chalk and cheese," states Alex. "Matt is a quiet man. If ever he wanted to give you advice or pass criticism he would call you aside and have a word or two in private.

"Doc tends to shout at you, publicly single you out. But all the players respect him, realising it's all part of his nature and that it's good for us in the long run, anyway.

"Actually, Tommy has mellowed over the years. I was at Chelsea when he was in charge and, believe me, he's changed considerably.

"Despite their different personalities and approaches to the game, Sir Matt and The Doc are friends and have enormous respect for one another."

NERVOUS START

Big Gordon McQueen (below), "Gogo" to his Leeds team-mates, is one of the last players in the country you would think was affected by nerves. Yet that wasn't always the case.

Alex Wright, the man who signed him for St. Mirren and who now bosses Dumbarton, reveals: "I'm certain no player has had a more soul-destroying start to his professional career than big Gordon.

"He made his debut for us in a friendly against Crystal Palace and they had their then-new £100,000 signing Alan Birchenall up against him.

"Gordon lasted precisely two minutes before we had to take him off—because he was so nervous he was physically sick!"

Dundee United paid out £40,000 for Dumbarton striker Tom McAdam in October, 1975 and Tannadice manager Jim McLean was suitably impressed when the player scored two goals in his debut match.

There is an odd note, though, about the transfer . . . at the start of the 1975-76 season Jim's brother Willie, the Motherwell boss, bought Colin McAdam from Dumbarton—and, of course, Colin is Tom's brother!

Thanks, Doog

Perseverance is a word which certainly applies to Birmingham City striker Peter Withe.

Before he had reached the end of his teens he had been discarded by Southport, Preston and Barrow.

He required a spell in South Africa, where he was spotted by former Northern Ireland international and Wolves star Derek Dougan, before he made any impact.

Peter, with Wolves before his £40,000 transfer to St. Andrews in June last year, said: "I can never hope to repay The Doog."

City's 'Roy of the Rovers'

From junior groundsman to First Division stardom. It sounds like "Roy of the Rovers" fiction, but for Manchester City's Ken Clements (left) it's a fairy tale come true.

Spotted playing for a Manchester Sunday League team, he signed amateur forms for City. But turning out for their junior sides on Saturdays lost him his job, so he was appointed to the groundsman's staff at the club's Cheadle training centre.

"I never thought that one day I would be playing in the First Division," says Ken, "although that is what happened."

During the summer of 1975 he was signed as a full professional at Maine Road, and at the age of 20 the former Manchester UNITED supporter was pitched into the first-team at right-back.

GEORGE PETCHEY — man of principle

You won't hear Orient manager George Petchey (below) get excited about the standard of refereeing, but he is one of the growing chorus who are concerned about the harsh treatment being handed out by over-physical players to some of the game's most skilful stars.

After one home win, Petchey defended his coaching methods. "I shall keep playing for the principles I believe in," he said.

"I admire talent, skill and character and I have to convince my players that is the way to win games.

"Unfortunately, there are too many hard, physical sides. They win matches and make people think THAT is the right way to play."

Well said, Mr. Petchey.

Headed spot-kick

Have you ever heard of a headed penalty? Several record books have credited former Arsenal and England captain Eddie Hapgood with one.

It happened at Liverpool in October, 1936 when goalkeeper Arthur Riley saved his shot and Hapgood headed in the rebound.

Last season it happened again when Nottingham Forest's John Robertson saw his spot-kick against Hull City saved by Jeff Wealands but flung himself forward to head the loose ball home.

PETER WITHE
BIRMINGHAM CITY

BRIAN KIDD
ARSENAL

15

MERSEYSIDE DERBIES

by MIKE LYONS

Everton defender Mike Lyons will never forget the Merseyside derby clash at Anfield in 1965-1966.

He was a fan at the time, and had the cheek to stand on the famous Liverpool Kop wearing a blue-and-white scarf.

Everton lost 5-0 and afterwards Mike was too choked to even discuss the game with his pals.

"There is only one feeling worse than *seeing* your team beaten in an Everton/Liverpool meeting.

"And that's *playing* for the side that's gone down. Believe me, that is a hundred times worse, especially for a local lad like myself."

Luckily, it's a feeling that Mike hasn't experienced very often . . . since he became an Everton regular, the derby games have, in the main, been draws, although Liverpool have the more victories.

"I've played in over half a dozen derbies now. It was frustrating not to be able to get the edge over Liverpool even if we weren't losing.

"It is often said that if Everton beat Liverpool but lose all their other games our fans won't worry.

"That's obviously an exaggeration . . . but there's some truth in it. When one side beats the other, the opposing fans are reminded of it until the next game.

"Rivalry is intense.

"But unlike some other two-club cities, our supporters aren't violent. Our fans are known for their humour, not their fists."

Then . . . an admission that may shock the blue half of Liverpool—and the red half, come to that.

"One of my best friends is Terry McDermott, who I've known for some years."

Earlier in his career, Mike was known as a "Mr. Versatility", being able to fill a number of roles with equal effect.

He formed a deadly striking partnership with £300,000 Bob Latchford in 1974/75 and the pair banged in 25 League goals between them.

Now, Mike seems to have settled down in the back-four alongside stopper Roger Kenyon.

"I still have plenty of scoring chances. I'm involved in most of our set-piece movements.

"Over the years, I've found that my goals come in patches. You know, three in four games then nothing for six games. Strange, isn't it?"

16

ABERDEEN's exciting raider Arthur Graham has one of the strangest titles in Scottish soccer—he surely must qualify as the youngest veteran in the game!

Graham has just turned 24, yet he has been playing in the Pittodrie first team for the past eight years. The Aberdeen fans accepted him immediately he was introduced to the team at outside-left by former manager Eddie Turnbull. Now fair-haired Arthur is as much a part of The Dons' scene as the Pittodrie goal-posts!

In his time Graham has played beside men such as Zoltan Varga, Stevie Murray, Joe Harper and Martin Buchan. He has watched as these players left for even bigger money—and he hasn't grumbled. He has got on with his game and matured into a fine, subtle player who can combine electrifying acceleration with shrewd promptings from the middle of the park.

"Graham is a real professional," says manager Ally MacLeod. "I remember one game a few years ago when he was playing against my former club, Ayr United.

"He had been switched to the midfield and he was absolutely unstoppable. I thought he was a good winger, but that night he proved he could be just as effective in another role.

"There are not a lot of young players around who can accept versatility such as this. Graham may be young in years, but he is old in experience and he has proved this. You don't just have to take my word for it."

Graham first exploded upon the soccer scene when he helped Aberdeen to an amazing Scottish Cup Final victory over Celtic when he was only 16. Graham, in fact,

Aberdeen's young 'veteran'

Arthur Graham comes from a family that traditionally supports Celtic. But that didn't stop him helping Aberdeen beat The Celts 3-1 in the 1970 Scottish Cup Final. Below, The Dons' defence defies Jimmy Johnstone.

offered his winner's medal to Aberdeen scout Bobby Calder, the man who spotted him and brought him to Pittodrie.

"I come from a large family," says Arthur, "all Celtic-mad! I'm not too sure whether or not they wanted Celtic or Aberdeen to win when we played in the Scottish Cup Final in 1970, and won 3-1!"

It is impossible to anticipate what quick-thinking Graham will do, he's so unpredictable.

Wing wonder? Or midfield maestro? Which does Graham prefer? His answer is typical of his refreshing enthusiasm for the game. He says: "So long as I am in the first team I don't mind. Mr. MacLeod is the man who makes the decision about who plays where."

Graham—the young veteran—has certainly proved his capabilities to everyone. His adaptability is astonishing; his footwork dazzling and his finishing lethal. No wonder he is known as King Arthur around Pittodrie!

RECORD WINS AND DEFEATS...

Middlesbrough 8   Sheffield Wed. 0
(Hickton, Murdoch, Mills,
Souness 3, Foggon 2)
April 20th, 1974

It was the last home game at Ayresome Park for the 1973-74 season. A campaign that had seen a runaway win of the Second Division Championship by the Middlesbrough club.

Jackie Charlton, in his first year as manager, had won promotion for a club which in recent years had always been so near, yet so far from success.

'Boro opponents were Sheffield Wednesday, desperately needing points to avoid relegation to Division Three.

But unfortunately for Wednesday, they met a Middlesbrough side determined to finish their home programme with a memorable victory.

Only six minutes had passed when John Hickton scored, in the 14th minute young David Mills made it two and veteran Bobby Murdoch, a great signing from Celtic, added the third in the 36th minute.

Three-up at half-time, but it gave no clue to the deluge that was to hit the Sheffield side after the interval.

Graeme Souness, snapped up by Jackie Charlton when he wanted to leave Tottenham, steamed in with a hat-trick and Alan Foggon hit two.

With a 4-2 win at Preston on the following Saturday, Middlesbrough won the Second Division by a massive 15 points. It was a happy finish for Wednesday, too, for they steered clear of relegation with a last match win.

Middlesbrough: Platt, Craggs, Spraggon, Souness, Boam, Maddren, Murdoch (Charlton H), Foggon, Mills, Hickton, Armstrong.
Sheff. Wed.: Springett, Rodriques, Shaw, Mullen, Holsgrove, Coyle, (Eustace), Potts, Craig (T), Joicey, Prudham, Cameron.

* On November 18th, 1933, Middlesbrough beat Sheffield United 10-3 in a Division One match. We selected the victory v Sheffield Wednesday because it has the greater goal-difference.

'Boro's Graeme Souness struck a memorable hat-trick against unfortunate Sheffield Wednesday.

Blackburn 9   Middlesbrough 0
(Quigley 3, Mooney 3,
Crossan 2, Langton)
November 6th, 1954

To prove that not all the fireworks were used the previous day, Blackburn gave Middlesbrough the heaviest-ever defeat on November 6th, 1954.

Blackburn were to score 114 goals this season, although they could only finish 6th in Division Two, while 'Boro ended 12th.

One notable absentee from the scoring spree was Tommy Briggs, who finished with 33 League goals for Rovers. But quicksilver Eddie Quigley scored three towards a season's total of 28. Also with a hat-trick was Frank Mooney; Eddie Crossan got two and England winger Bobby Langton hit the other goal.

It was a devastating display of scoring by Blackburn against a team far from weak. At centre-forward was Charlie Wayman, a new signing from Preston, who was to score 16 for the Teesside club. The half-back line of Bill Harris, Dick Robinson and Ronnie Dicks was a fine one. But they were no match for Rovers.

Blackburn: Elvy, Stuart, Eckersley, Clayton, Kelly, Bell, Mooney, Crossan, Briggs, Quigley, Langton.
Middlesbrough: Ugolini, Barnard, Brown, Harris, Robinson, Dicks, Delepenha, Scott, Wayman, Fitzsimmons, Mitchell.

# of four famous First Division clubs

West Ham 8   Rotherham 0
Dick 4, Keeble 2, Smith 2)
March 8th, 1958

Twice the FA Cup and also European Cup-Winners' Cup glory has come to Upton Park since the 1957-58 season.

But West Ham fans still remember the Second Division promotion side with affection.

Like latter-day Hammer sides, they also believed the best soccer was to attack their opponents' goal and they certainly went about it in style the year they won the Second Division Championship.

West Ham scored 101 goals. And in a season which was as hard-fought as anyone can remember, they finished a point in front of runners-up Blackburn who themselves won a dramatic last game against third-placed Charlton to pip the London club of promotion.

Big John Dick, who was to score four against Rotherham, finished top scorer with 21 League goals, while Vic Keeble, a brilliant capture from Newcastle netted 19. Vic got a brace in this match as also did John Smith in West Ham's new record victory.

West Ham: Gregory, Bond, Wright, Malcolm, Brown, Lansdowne, Grice, Smith, Keeble, Dick, Musgrove.
Rotherham: Quairney, Silman, Morgan, Williams, Noble, Keyworth, Webster, Kettleborough, Twidle, Jones, Broadbent.

West Ham 8   Sunderland 0
(Hurst 6, Moore, Brooking)
October 19th, 1968

West Ham's record score of 1958 was to last only ten years, yet when it was equalled it was completely unexpected.

West Ham had gone nine games without a win and the near-25,000 crowd just hoped to see The Hammers triumph at long last.

They got their victory, and they also saw Geoff Hurst equal the club's individual scoring record which had stood since 1929.

World Cup Final hero Geoff had his finest-ever scoring day for The Hammers when he netted six goals.

Skipper Bobby Moore and a young Trevor Brooking scored the other two.

West Ham: Ferguson, Bonds, Charles, Peters, Stephenson, Moore, Redknapp, Boyce, Brooking, Hurst, Sissons.
Sunderland: Montgomery, Irwin, Palmer, Hurley, Harvey, Porterfield, Herd, Harris, Brand, Suggett, Mulhall.

Blackburn Rovers' Andy McEvoy scored three goals on the Boxing Day that West Ham want to forget.

West Ham 2   Blackburn Rovers 8
(Byrne 2)   (Pickering 3,
                          McEvoy 3, Douglas,
                          Ferguson)
December 26th, 1963

Boxing Day soccer is notorious for throwing up weird results, and one was at Upton Park when visitors Blackburn inflicted West Ham's heaviest-ever defeat.

Fred Pickering and Don McEvoy led the way with hat-tricks. Bryan Douglas and Mike Ferguson completed the rout.

Yet two days later, showing only one change, Eddie Bovington for Martin Peters, West Ham went to Ewood Park for the return match and won 3-1 !

West Ham: Standen, Bond, Burkett, Peters, Brown, Moore, Brabrook, Boyce, Byrne, Hurst, Sissons.
Blackburn: Else, Bray, Newton, Clayton, England, McGrath, Ferguson, McEvoy, Pickering, Douglas, Harrison.

RECORD WINS AND DEFEATS...

Four goals from Man. United's Dennis Viollet helped to demolish unhappy Anderlecht.

Manchester United 10   Anderlecht 0
(Viollet 4, Taylor 3,
Whelan 2, Berry)
September 26th, 1956

The Busby Babes were wonderful. Those who were lucky to see them in action can still shut their eyes and remember, although nearly 20 years have passed since the Munich air crash.

The calm authority of skipper Roger Byrne at full-back, the powerful thrust of wing-half Duncan Edwards, the greatest of the greats.

The full-blooded challenge of centre-forward Tommy Taylor. So much skill belonged to the eight stars who died as a result of that black day in Germany.

United were the first England side to enter the European Cup in 1956 and drawn against Anderlecht of Belgium they started the Preliminary Round with an impressive away win 2–0.

In the return at Maine Road (Old Trafford was then without floodlights), they showed their greatness. In torrential rain, they were a class apart. Outstanding passing and non-stop power shooting and accuracy.

It took the magic of Real Madrid to knock United out in the Semi-Finals 5–3 on aggregate.

Man. Utd: Wood, Foulkes, Byrne, Coleman, Jones, Edwards, Berry, Whelan, Taylor, Viollet, Pegg.
Anderlecht: Week, Gettemans, Culot, Van der Wilt, De Koster, Hanon, De Drijver, Van Der Bosch, Mermans, De Wael, Juion.

Aston Villa 7   Manchester United 0
(Mandley 2, Houghton (2 pens),
Brown 2, Beresford)
December 27th, 1930

Aston Villa did not win the League or FA Cup in the 1930–31 season, but they did set up a record that stands even today.

As fans love goals, it is a record that thrilled crowds all over the country as Villa crashed in 128 goals to create a new First Division record. But even that grand total was not to win them the title—they finished runners-up to Arsenal.

Manchester United's heaviest defeat at Villa Park was just another score as far as Villa fans were concerned. That season they beat Champions-to-be Arsenal 5–1, Middlesbrough were swamped 8–1 and Huddersfield were beaten home and away 6–1, while at Upton Park they shared a 10-goal thriller 5–5.

Goals flowed from the feet of 'Pongo' Waring who this season hit 49, Eric Houghton 30, Billy Walker 16 and Joe Beresford 13.

But for United it was to be a different kind of season. They finished bottom of Division One, conceding 115 goals. They were to lose at home 7–4 to Newcastle and Huddersfield 6–0. Away from home they generously let in goals.

Villa and United met on the third day of the Christmas programme. Villa had won 2–0 at Chelsea and drew 3–3 at Villa Park in the return. United had lost at home 3–1 and drew 1–1 at Stamford Bridge.

But that 7–0 beating at Villa Park is one record that Tommy Docherty will not want to be beaten.

A. Villa: Maggs, Smart, Mort, Gibson, Talbot, Tate, Mandley, Beresford, Brown, Walker, Houghton.
Man. Utd.: Stewarth, Mellor, Dale, Bennion, Hilditch, Wilson, Ramsden, Gallimore, Reid, Rowley, McLachlan.

Leeds 10   Lyn Oslo 0
(Jones 3, Clarke 2,
Giles 2, Bremner 2,
O'Grady)
September 17th, 1969

Leeds were Champions of the Football League for the first time in the club's history.

For the previous three seasons they had played in Europe while contesting the Fairs Cup, but this was their first crack at the major European trophy.

So on September 17th, the faithful at Elland Road gathered to watch Lyn Oslo of Norway supply the opposition in the First Round, First Leg.

It was not expected to be a hard task, but the ease with which Leeds disposed of the Norwegians was enough to set up a new Leeds record score.

The match turned into a shoot-in for the goal-happy Leeds strikers.

Poor Olsen in the visitors' goal tried valiantly to stop what must have seemed an avalanche.

Skipper Billy Bremner joined in with two from midfield as did jinking genius Johnny Giles. Mike O'Grady scored one and those goal twins of Allan Clarke (2) and Mick Jones (3) supplied the hammer punch.

Leeds: Sprake, Reaney, Cooper, Bremner, Charlton, Hunter, Madeley, Clarke, Jones, Giles, (Bates), O'Grady.

Lyn Oslo: Olsen (S), Rodvang, Oestvold, Morisbak, Kolle, Gulden, Borrehaug, Christophersen, Berg, Olsen (O), (Havdan), Austnes.

Stoke City 8   Leeds United 1
(Matthews 4, Johnson 2,   (Hornby)
Sale 2)
August 27th, 1934

The 1934–35 season had opened on August 25th and First Division Leeds had been stunned when Middlesbrough went to Elland Road and won 4–2. But another team to concede four on the same day were Stoke City as Sheffield Wednesday beat them 4–1 at Hillsborough.

So Leeds went to Stoke two days later not unduly worried about meeting City. After all, Stoke were comparative newcomers to Division One, after finishing Champions of Division Two in the 1932–33 season, and been 12th in their first season back in the First.

What a surprise the Victoria Ground side had in store for Leeds. They ran riot and ended as 8–1 winners.

It was a good Stoke side—Stanley Matthews had won his first England cap the previous season—and the young Stan was a bit of a goalscorer in those days. In that season he scored 10 goals, with four against Leeds, and was joint second top scorer behind Ted Sale who scored 25 goals. Frank Soo and Freddie Steele were also beginning fine careers with City.

But despite that 8–1 hammering, Leeds escaped relegation as they finished 18th while Stoke were to end 10th.

Stoke: Scattergood, McGrory, Spencer, Tutin, Turner, Sellars, Matthews, Davies, Sale, Liddle, Johnson.

Leeds: Moore, Milburn (J), Milburn (G), Edwards, Hart, Hornby, Cochrane, Mills, Firth, Furness, Worsley.

Mick Jones (background, left) hit a superb hat-trick for Leeds in their 10-0 win over Lyn Oslo.

'no short-

IT doesn't take young players coming into the game at senior level long to learn that there is no quick road to the top.

Naturally, some youngsters possess more basic skills than others, but that doesn't mean that the more talented players don't have to work just as hard.

I suppose quite a few lads with stars in their eyes have had their illusions of stardom shattered simply because they thought that once they had been signed by a senior club a lot of the hard work was behind them.

Believe me, when you are called up by a League club the real work is only just beginning—and a regular first-team place is still a long way off.

Frankly, I didn't have any illusions shattered when I joined Celtic as a full-timer at the age of 17. I was grateful to be given the chance to become a professional with such a great club.

But like most youngsters I was thrilled to be training alongside so many big name players.

When I was called up to Parkhead in July, 1968, Celtic held the European Cup, having beaten Inter-Milan 2-1 in the Final in Lisbon. So, the team at that time was the toast of Europe.

There was nothing big-headed about the "Lisbon Lions". Despite their tremendous success they were friendly and always willing to give tips and encouragement to the young players.

It was in October, 1969, at the age of 18, that I made my first-team debut against Raith Rovers in a League match at Parkhead. We won, and I was delighted, although I knew there was still a long way to go before I became firmly established.

For playing top team football is different from playing for the reserves. You've got to learn to pace yourself over 90 minutes and time tackles, aspects of the game that come from experience.

Obviously, very few players break through into first-team football and stay there. Usually you are given a taste of what it's like and allowed to progress gradually, playing a few games and then being rested to ensure that you adjust properly.

Eventually, when a player does become a recognised first-team man, there is going to come a time when he is "dropped". Nobody enjoys that happening to them.

Still, there are only 11 places on offer at any one time and no manager can afford to keep playing anyone

cut to success'

who hits a form slump, especially if he has an in-form player ready to step in.

On the occasions when I have been "dropped" no one has told me the reasons why. They don't have to. Any player worth his salt knows it's due to loss of form.

Don't ask me why it happens. One week you can play brilliantly, the next have a right "stinker". It's all part and parcel of the game.

Mind you, when a player goes through a sticky patch it isn't because he's not working hard at the game. You can give one hundred percent and still find that things just don't come off for you.

Sometimes I am asked "Is there any part of your game that you would like to improve on?" The answer to that is, yes . . . everything.

I reckon once you feel you know it all and think you can do it all, it's time to hang up your boots.

You're always learning in this game, no matter whether you are 18 and a new arrival on the First Division scene, or 30 and starting to approach the end of your career.

I have been playing regular first-team football for almost seven years, yet I know I am no "Dixie Deans" in the air or "David Hay" in the tackle.

This may surprise you, but my main aim as a football player is not to win everything in sight, although hopefully I will continue to enjoy a lot of success with Celtic, but to gain the respect and friendship of my fellow professionals—managers and players alike. I believe that to be the highest honour a player can achieve.

It's not something which comes easily. You've got to prove that you are dedicated and sportsmanlike in your outlook.

International football is, of course, a bonus, an extra which comes from playing well for your club. It is also an honour for the club and yourself.

I love playing for my country. There's something special about pulling on an international shirt in the knowledge that millions are rooting for you.

On the subject of international football, I don't have to tell you who my favourite Scotland star was. Yes, "The King" himself, Denis Law.

I know I have talked about him before in *Shoot/Goal*, but I make no apology for doing so again, because Denis was, to my mind, one of the greatest of all time.

Although Denis was a tremend-ously gifted player, who appeared to possess just about all the skills, he didn't reach the top without a lot of hard work.

When Denis went from his home in Aberdeen to England as a young-ster a lot of people questioned Huddersfield's wisdom in signing him because of his frail build. But he silenced the doubters in double-quick time by striving to become a true professional. It pays to remember that.

There's no short-cut to success!

All the best for now.

Kenny Dalglish

Kenny resists a challenge by Denmark's Neils Sorensen in an international match. (Below) His favourite Scotland player—'The King' himself—Denis Law.

23

Qualifying for The World Cup Finals –
HOW THINGS HAVE CHANGED!

The hundred and six of FIFA's 140-plus member countries entered for the next World Cup, but within days of the draw it was announced that Sri Lanka, formerly Ceylon, had been expelled because their entrance fee had not been received by the due date.

From the record field of 106 entrants, more will surely follow Sri Lanka if the past is anything to go by. For economic or political reasons, several more countries will drop out, mostly from amongst the developing countries of Asia, Africa and Central America. But it was not always like this and qualifying rounds were not always held.

Indeed, for the first World Cup series, staged in Montevideo, in 1930, almost anyone who could raise a team and reserves with sufficient time off work to make the long journey by sea would have been welcomed. Finally, only 13 teams took part, including four from Europe—France, Belgium, Yugoslavia and, somewhat surprisingly, Rumania, where the King intervened personally to persuade employers of the players to give them the

necessary time off without loss of pay while the government paid the expenses.

One of the big surprises amongst those 13 who gave the World Cup its start 46 years ago was the U.S.A. Not the professional players who take part now but real amateurs, mostly European immigrants, and to everyone's surprise they did very well. The only English-speaking team in that first World Cup, the United States beat Belgium 3-0 and Paraguay 3-0 to reach the Semi-Finals!

In 1934 qualifying matches were needed for the first time when Italy played host and 30 countries, including 21 from Europe, took part. Very few of the qualifying matches were actually played and for example Chile and Peru both withdrew when the F.I.F.A. draw ordained they were to play qualifying matches against the much stronger Argentina and Brazil. Another strange feature was the qualifying tie between Egypt (now the United Arab Republic) and Palestine (now Israel) and for the first time the Republic of Ireland (Eire) took part, the only

Only 13 teams took part in the very first World Cup competition, held in Uruguay. The host nation won the Final against Argentina by 4-2. Shown here is a goal scored by the Uruguyan player Hector Castro.

team from the British Isles. The U.S.A. were there once more, crossing the Atlantic to Italy where 17 teams assembled for 16 places. Three days before the series proper, began, the U.S.A. beat Mexico 4-2 in a final qualifying match and Mexico went home after playing only one game.

In those far-off days, however, there were no qualifying groups in the final stages. Everyone

played on a tie-by-tie knockout basis so that after the first round, eight other countries had also been eliminated after one game only. Twenty eight countries entered for the 1938 World Cup in France, two less than in 1934, but one more country from Europe, represented originally by 22 countries.

Eire were there again, but once more the system used was the one-game knockout until only two were left to play the Final. Little Austria had been amongst the original 28 entrants but having been occupied by Nazi Germany they withdrew, giving Sweden a bye.

After that it was twelve years before another World Cup could be staged with World War Two intervening. But the original Cup, now held by Brazil who won it outright under the old rules in 1970 by winning the competition three times, was not forgotten. When Italy who won the 1934 and 1938 competitions, withdrew from the War, their FA officials dutifully buried the trophy and kept its whereabouts secret from the Germans who immediately occupied Northern Italy with orders to take old works of art, and objects of precious metals and put them on trains

(Left) the 1938 Final was held in Paris, Italy beating Hungary. Italy's Rava heads clear. (Below) The victorious Italians celebrate their successful defence of the trophy, having won it in the previous 1934 tournament in Italy.

bound for Germany.

By 1950 when the competition was next staged in Brazil one would have expected a massive field and fierce competition. England, Scotland, Ireland and Wales were back in the fold as F.I.F.A. members. But only 28 countries entered, this time with only 14 teams from Europe because Eastern Europe, under the rule of Stalin and the U.S.S.R., declined to take part.

Brazil (as host country) and Italy (as the holders) qualified automatically but as the final stages loomed a shambles began. Two places were allocated to Great Britain where the British Home Championship was used as the qualifying round. But the Scottish FA announced that they would only go to Brazil as British Champions, not as runners-up. England duly won the Home Championship and Scotland could not be persuaded to take part in the Finals. France were invited to go but said "no". Argentina also withdrew, having been placed in a group with Chile and Bolivia who were both invited to play in the final stages.

The U.S.A. had been eliminated 6-0 and 6-2 by Mexico, but they were invited to fill one of the gaps and did so. Turkey qualified but then withdrew and Portugal, who had been eliminated by Spain, were invited by F.I.F.A. but refused to travel. The result was that for the first time since qualifying games had been necessary only 13 teams instead of 16 finally appeared in Brazil.

For the first time F.I.F.A. had organized the competition for the first round on the lines used today. Urged by many countries who had travelled half way round the world to play only one game and be knocked out, F.I.F.A. introduced First Round Groups. In Groups 1 and 2 there were four finalists; in Group 3 there were only 3 and in Group 4 only Uruguay, the eventual winners, and Bolivia turned up.

After all the problems created as teams withdrew and replacements could not be found, there were still two major surprises to come. This was the competition in which the United States beat England 1-0 at Belo Horizonte to

as the qualifying round for United Kingdom teams and this time England and Scotland flew to Switzerland.

England reached the Quarter-Finals after being held to a 4-4 draw by Belgium but went out to Uruguay who had earlier thrashed Scotland 7-0. Half the Uruguayan team were veterans of their Rio triumph four years earlier but it was an unhappy time for Scotland whose manager resigned during the competition.

From a football point of view, however, perhaps this was the World Cup peak with a Semi-Final encounter between Hungary and Uruguay providing what many who were there that day in Lausanne, still claim was the best football they have ever seen. Hungary won 4-2 after extra time, but, unbeaten for five years, went on to lose 3-2 in the Final with West Germany.

Now it was Sweden's turn to play host in 1958 and the World

create a shock that shook the world. Then in the last game in a final pool created by the four original group winners, little Uruguay beat Brazil 2-1 to take the trophy. Brazil, at home in the huge 250,000 capacity Maracana stadium in Rio de Janeiro, were great favourites. With an inside-forward trio of Zizinho, Ademir and Jair, rated by many to be the finest the world had ever seen, they scored six goals in their other final pool games against Spain and Sweden and were 1-0 up against Uruguay. After the Final, several Brazilians committed suicide, while more died from heart attacks . . . and worst of all, several Uruguayans were murdered in Rio that night.

Four years later in 1954, Switzerland played host and there was a new record entry of 37 countries with 27 from Europe. Russia again stood aloof, but for example Czechoslovakia and Hungary—the latter as 1952 Olympic Games soccer Champions—took part from Eastern Europe. Once more the British Home Championship was used

In 1958, Brazil went to Sweden and captured the Cup for the first time, beating the host nation by five goals to two. A young Pele scored twice, and above is shown one of his great goals.

Bobby Moore proudly holds the gold trophy aloft as he and his team-mates come off the Wembley pitch after beating West Germany 4-2 in the 1966 Final. Another win for the host nation.

Pele turns jubilantly away after scoring a goal against Italy in the 1970 Final. Brazil's third Final win ensured they kept the trophy for all time.

Cup became a true *world* competition with a field of 50 entrants. For the first time, too, the British Associations played foreign teams in their qualifying groups and all four, England, Scotland, Northern Ireland and Wales, played in Sweden. The first three qualified in their groups, Ireland eliminating Italy who were one of the favourites, but Wales got in through the back door . . . and then went on to reach the Quarter-Finals !

Wales had been eliminated from a group won by Czechoslovakia, but because all the African and Asian teams refused to play against Israel for political reasons, F.I.F.A. asked them to play at home and away against Israel . . . and Wales won 2-0 and 2-0.

The 1962 series was played in Chile and 55 countries entered. Once more Europe provided the backbone with 28 entrants. Football penetrated the Iron Curtain and this time even the Russians took part and qualified. Indeed it was another East European country, Czechoslovakia, who reached the Final and took the lead before losing 3-2 to Brazil.

In 1966 it was England's turn to play host and win. Now the field zoomed to a record 72 countries with 33 from Europe—including Albania for the first time. But again politics intervened and all 15 African countries withdrew.

In addition South Korea refused to play North Korea and the Australian Government refused to grant visas to the North Koreans. Eventually Australia played North Korea over two games in neutral Cambodia for a place in the last 16.

Now the football world really began to expand as the decolonised countries of Africa and Asia began to develop their football. The qualifying competitions became more and more complex with 92 entrants for the 1974 series in West Germany and 106 entering for 1978. The new countries of Africa and Asia began demanding a bigger say in what went on and more places in the last 16. Eventually Africa and Asia will both get more than one place each and they will surely develop in the playing sense too.

It probably will not come in 1978 or even 1982, but the day cannot be very far away when the World Cup is won by an African or Asian country and end the domination of Europe and South America.

In the qualifying rounds for the 1978 series F.I.F.A. have once again followed their practice of ''seeding'' the teams from Europe and South America that qualified last time. Just how dangerous a practice this can be—and how unfair it is—is underlined by the 1974 draw. Then, England were placed in a group with Poland who had no previous World Cup ''form''. England were the seeded team expected to qualify again. This however took no account of the improvement the Poles had made, nor of the fact that they were the 1972 Olympic Games Soccer Champions.

In another 1974 qualifying group, Belgium (who qualified for 1970) were the seeded country, grouped with Holland. Belgium and England went out while the unseeded Holland went on to reach the Final with Poland occupying third place. Clearly the F.I.F.A. organisers need a new seeding system but for 1978 they have stuck to their old line. This has once more provided what can only be described as an unbalanced and unfair draw. In 1974 it was Russia's group that was chosen and it will be remembered they declined to play Chile and went out. This is not a bid to raise sympathy for the Russians but once more F.I.F.A. have ruled that the winners of Europe Group 9 (probably Russia) MUST meet a South American team for a place in the last 16.

Again, having made an error by pairing Holland (the 1974 Finalists) with Belgium who ended their group level on points, F.I.F.A. have done it again. Belgium can fairly claim that having equalled Holland on points and drawn twice (0-0) against the Dutch, they would have done well in the final stages had they qualified.

Similarly, in England's 1978 qualifying group there are Italy who, for all their recent difficulties have won the World Cup twice and have a fine record overall. Here it is Italy who are the seeded country and England the outsiders !

Clearly, with so much pressure for only 16 final places F.I.F.A. have a problem but a little commonsense should prevail over seeding systems that have been proved morally wrong.

In two other European Groups for the 1978 competition there are only weak teams who have done nothing for years in the international arena and are most unlikely to improve. Particularly, these are the two groups . . . with the 'seed' in capitals . . . BULGARIA, France, Eire. SWEDEN, Switzerland, Norway.

England (or Italy) would almost certainly beat both these seeded countries and the draw would have been much more sensible if England, Italy, Belgium and Holland had been separated and spread around the groups with Finland, Luxembourg, Iceland, Northern Ireland and the teams in the Bulgaria and Sweden groups.

EDUCATED

BELOW
Despite studying at Liverpool University, Steve Coppell managed to combine his brains with his boots. He has not been able to train regularly with his Manchester United team-mates, although his form never suffered through his absence from the day-to-day involvement.

ABOVE . . . West Ham and England midfield star Trevor Brooking passed no less than 15 subjects in his "O" and "A" levels.
BELOW . . . Leeds United's star striker Duncan McKenzie can boast ten "O" levels as well as considerable soccer talent.

FEET

BELOW
Liverpool schemer Brian Hall gained a science degree at Liverpool University. While he was studying, Brian used to work as a bus conductor during the summer!

ABOVE . . . Newcastle goal-getter Alan Gowling (stripes) was a part-time professional with Manchester United while he was studying for a B.A. economics degree. Alan became a full-time pro after passing.

BELOW . . . Graduated at Warwick University with an economics degree—that's Steve Heighway the Liverpool and Republic of Ireland winger. Steve talks about football as well as he plays it, which is brilliantly!

SOCCER NEWS THAT HIT THE HEADLINES

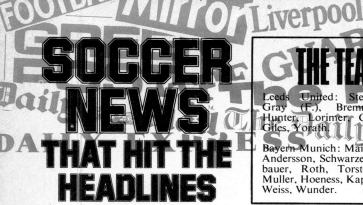

THE TEAMS

Leeds United: Stewart, Reaney, Gray (F.), Bremner, Madeley, Hunter, Lorimer, Clarke, Jordan, Giles, Yorath.

Bayern Munich: Maier, Durnberger, Andersson, Schwarzenbeck, Beckenbauer, Roth, Torstensson, Zobel, Muller, Hoeness, Kapellmann. Subs: Weiss, Wunder.

Leeds United (0) 0, Bayern Munich (0) 2
Parc des Princes stadium, Paris
May 28th, 1975

Attendance: 50,000

Leeds United, so often hit by misfortune when success seemed within their grasp, were robbed of the glittering prize that had been their dream and ambition for ten years — the European Cup.

For an hour of a disappointing Final they completely dominated Bayern Munich.

But after having at least one valid penalty-appeal turned down, and what they thought a perfectly good goal ruled out, Leeds allowed the West Germans to score twice to keep the trophy for the second year in succession.

However, the worst feature of the match wasn't Leeds United's defeat, but the disgraceful behaviour of a few thousand of their fans.

They tore up seats and pelted the Bayern penalty-area with beer cans and bottles throughout

Fans shame Leeds as Bayern keep the Cup

The European Cup trophy is safely in the hands of Bayern Munich goalkeeper Sepp Maier.

the last quarter of the game.

The sight of riot police moving in to throw out the hooligans sickened the players, officials and all true fans, not only in the stadium but throughout Europe.

The mob even forced Bayern to abandon the traditional victors' lap of honour at the end.

The West Germans won because they played a waiting game. They soaked up every-

thing Leeds threw at them before suddenly launching their own counter-attacks and delivering the killer blows.

From the first whistle, Leeds went hunting for goals. Joe Jordan was particularly danger-ous in the air, causing Schwarzenbeck all sorts of problems.

Then Bayern lost a key man when Bjorn Andersson was car-ried off with a leg injury after a tackle by Terry Yorath.

Four minutes later, French referee Michel Kitabdjian booked Paul Reaney for a foul on Uli Hoeness, who also had to leave the field just before half-time following a clash with Yorath.

Then, in the 38th minute, Franz "Emperor" Beckenbauer ap-peared to trip Allan Clarke from behind close to the byeline. The referee waved aside all protests from Leeds for what looked a blatant penalty.

Billy Bremner, often the inspir-

ation behind many a Leeds triumph, could well have won the European Cup for them in the 65th minute.

Peter Lorimer took a free-kick on the left that was flicked on by Paul Madeley to Billy Bremner inside the six-yard box.

With the goal at his mercy, the Leeds skipper shot straight into the arms of 'keeper Sepp Maier.

One minute later Leeds had a goal disallowed.

A flick from Johnny Giles—superb in midfield—was only half-cleared by a German defen-der and the ball found Lorimer who smashed it into the net.

Instead of a goal, referee Kitabdjian awarded a free-kick to Bayern. Afterwards he claimed Bremner had been fractionally offside.

Five minutes later the moment the West Germans had been waiting for arrived and FRANZ ROTH collected a pass from Tortensson to shoot wide of 'keeper David Stewart.

Not long after, with pande-monium raging in the stadium, Norman Hunter and then Frankie Gray failed to stop Josef Kapell-mann from making a penetrating dash down the right.

From his pass, GERD MULLER, who had been kept quiet throughout the game, lived up to his reputation as the most lethal finisher in Europe by driving a tremendous left-foot shot past Stewart.

There was nothing Leeds could do to save a match they should have won long before—a game they dominated from start to finish.

As one English journalist put it at the end : "Leeds always looked like winning until they lost."

Skipper Billy Bremner fails to beat Sepp Maier from close range. Shortly after-wards, Leeds had a goal disallowed.

AFTER-MATCH COMMENTS

Jimmy Armfield, Leeds manager : "There were two distinct mom-ents which turned the game in Bayern's favour. I thought it was a definite penalty when Becken-bauer tripped Allan Clarke in the first half. And things went against us once more in the

Continued on page 32

SOCCER NEWS THAT HIT THE HEADLINES CONTINUED

second half when Maier was able to bring off that vital save from Billy Bremner."

Dettmar Cramer, Bayern manager:

"I am happy to win the Cup again, but my feelings are mixed. I am unhappy about the manner in which two of my best players, Hoeness and Andersson, received bad injuries."

Billy Bremner, Leeds skipper:

"To say I'm disappointed is putting it mildly. I'm utterly sick for myself, my team-mates and the whole of Leeds. This was to have been the most wonderful night of my career, instead it was a dream that ended in a nightmare. As for those mindless morons who ran riot during and after the match—I hate them. I was criticised for leading the team over to applaud our supporters at the end. People completely misunderstood what we did. Most of the hooligans had left or had been thrown out. We were thanking the genuine fans that were left for following us not only to Paris but all over Europe."

Franz Beckenbauer, Bayern captain:

"Lucky, Bayern? No! We knew if we played a waiting game, that sooner or later Leeds would overreach themselves and leave gaps at the back. Then we would be able to counter-attack, and score, and Leeds, being the older team, would not have the stamina to come back at us again. We scored two good goals and survived the loss of two players, injured as a result of violent tackles."

> Wrecked seats litter the pitch as French riot police face an angry mob of Leeds supporters during the game. Scenes like this brought disgrace to a fine club...it must never be allowed to happen again.

> Three European Finals in four years have been marred by crowd trouble.
> 1972—Cup-Winners' Cup, Rangers v. Moscow Dynamo in Barcelona.
> 1974—U.E.F.A. Cup. Spurs v. Feyenoord in Rotterdam.
> 1975—European Cup, Leeds v. Bayern Munich in Paris.

HOW THEY REACHED THE FINAL

Leeds United

First Round

Leeds	4	FC Zurich	1
Clarke (2),		Katic	
Jordan,			
Lorimer (pen)			

FC Zurich	2	Leeds	1
Katic,		Clarke	
Rutschmann (pen)			

(Leeds won 5-3 on aggregate)

Second Round

Ujpest Dozsa	1	Leeds	2
Fazekas (pen)		Lorimer,	
		McQueen	

Leeds	3	Ujpest Dozsa	0
McQueen,			
Bremner,			
Yorath			

(Leeds won 5-1 on aggregate)

Quarter-Final

Leeds	3	Anderlecht	0
Jordan,			
McQueen,			
Lorimer			

Anderlecht	0	Leeds	1
		Bremner	

(Leeds won 4-0 on aggregate)

Semi-Final

Leeds	2	Barcelona	1
Bremner,		Ascensi	
Clarke			

Barcelona	1	Leeds	1
Clares		Lorimer	

(Leeds won 3-2 on aggregate)

Bayern Munich

First Round

Bye

Second Round

Bayern Munich	3	1.FC	

Muller (2)		Magdeburg	2
Enge (o.g.)		Hansen (o.g.),	
1.FC		Sparwasser	

Magdeburg	1	Bayern Munich	2
Sparwasser		Muller (2)	

(Bayern won 5-3 on aggregate)

Quarter-Final

Bayern Munich	2	Ararat Erewan	0
Hoeness,			
Torstensson			

Ararat Erewan	1	Bayern Munich	0
Andreassjan			

(Bayern won 2-1 on aggregate)

Semi-Final

St. Etienne	0	Bayern Munich	0

Bayern Munich	2	St. Etienne	0
Beckenbauer			
Durnberger			

(Bayern won 2-0 on aggregate)

Times were when the West Ham crowd used to boo Pat Holland. As The Hammers struggled to stay alive in Division One, young Pat was trying to establish himself in the side. Not the ideal time . . .

Now, of course, West Ham are once again a top team. They've added bite to their skill and the result is a very attractive but difficult to beat outfit.

One of the stars is Pat Holland and the local lad bears no grudges against the Upton Park boo-boys.

He says: "I must confess that it hurt at the time. It was only a small section of the crowd, anyway.

"I think we have one of the most loyal sets of fans in England. Even during the bad times they never deserted us.

"It was a challenge for me to win them over. I like to think I've succeeded."

Pat points out another reason why he took so long to make a first-team place his own.

"Many people consider being versatile is a blessing. I disagree. Because I could play either in midfield, on the wing or as a striker, I didn't have the opportunity to settle down in one particular position.

"Looking back, I think this could have gone against me.

"My favourite position is in the centre of the middle three, but this is where Trevor Brooking operates. He is so consistent that

his place. I have no complaints . . . it was the right decision."

Pat, a professional for almost eight years, was suddenly a star. Now, 18 months later, with around 150 League games to his credit, he is one of the most accomplished forwards in Division One.

West Ham score a lot of goals from midfield, where Pat likes to play, but he is quick to praise the strikers.

"As front-men, they are expected to score. When fans see other players on the score-sheet, some think the strikers haven't done their job.

"In fact, our recognised goalmen do a lot of work off the ball creating space for the rest of the side.

"And, of course, it doesn't matter who scores . . . as long as somebody does."

Born in nearby Poplar, Pat used to support West Ham as a boy.

"I don't think there is any extra pressure on local-born players," he says. "After all, everyone is expected to pull his full weight."

Pat is a rival for team-mate Trevor Brooking's position—in the centre of the midfield trio.

'BEING VERSATILE IS A DRAWBACK'
says West Ham's PAT HOLLAND

there is no chance of anyone displacing him!

"I'm just happy to be in the team. I feel I'm more established now, although when I look at some of the players who wear our substitute's jersey, I realise just how much competition there is."

Pat also reflects on the loan period he had at Bournemouth a few years ago.

"No disrespect to them, but the Fourth Division was an eye-

opener. The midfield hardly exists, with so many long balls pumped upfield.

"Playing at that level did me good. I realised how important it was that I made the grade with West Ham."

Pat's biggest moment came in May, 1975, when John Lyall told him that he'd be playing in the F.A. Cup Final.

Bobby Gould, named as sub, showed the spirit of West Ham by saying: "Pat fully deserves

DAVE NEEDHAM

NOTTS COUNTY

ALAN BIRCHENALL
LEICESTER CITY

MATCH DAY

"There's a simple reason why it won't blow, sir. Someone's put a sock in it."

"I want to make an early start in the morning."

"I'm going now, dear. Where's my hat?"

TONY POWELL
NORWICH CITY

MIKE PEJIC

STOKE CITY

WORLD WIDE

compiled by
CHRIS DAVIES

No fun for Brigitte...

Watching your husband play football can be rather unsettling. Opponents don't always treat him with respect . . . especially if he's a big-name star.

Bayern Munich and West Germany captain Franz Beckenbauer certainly comes into this category and his pretty wife, Brigitte, seems anxious about his welfare.

She needn't have worried. Once again "The Emperor" led his team to victory with another first-class performance.

The strange story of soccer's most famous father-in-law

The most famous father-in-law in European soccer is Cor Coster. Mr. Coster was already a rich man through his diamond interests.

When his daughter, Danny, married a certain Johan Cruyff, Coster's business empire entered a new dimension.

He became Cruyff's agent and made his son-in-law rich. The big pay-off came when Coster organised a near £1 million transfer of Cruyff to Barcelona.

This brought Ajax a tidy sum,

...or Franz's dummies!

Here's Franz, himself, training with some new "team-mates". The dummies are used as a defensive wall for Bayern's free-kick experts to practise bending kicks round.

Looks like a Bayern player has been busy drawing a face!

Cruyff and his wife became financially secure . . . and it's a fair bet that Coster's bank manager wore a wide grin.

Coster's next transfer dealing was also from Ajax to Barcelona — Johan Neeskens. Again, a lot of money was involved for all parties. Then . . . Johnny Rep to Valencia for a six-figure fee.

Things were going so well for Coster that he decided to set-up his own agency, Inter-Football, with former Ajax star Piet Keizer and journalist Maarten de Vos as co-directors.

Almost 50 Dutch players signed contracts with Inter-Football, giving them exclusive rights to represent the players in all matters. For a good percentage, of course.

Business was booming. Several more players were transferred through Inter-Football and commercial deals brought in extra cash.

Then, the Dutch F.A. and Players' Union started to get upset. "This money belongs to us," they claimed. "It should be kept in football."

So, the Dutch authorities opened their own transfer-office and banned Inter-Football from acting as agents. Giving advice, however, was still allowed.

Soon afterwards, Ajax bought a player called Ling and the player openly talked about Inter-Football's "help".

"No!" said Coster's agency. "We only advised. We didn't have anything to do with the transfer."

The Dutch F.A. didn't have a case, so Ling's transfer stood.

Even so, it was obvious that Inter-Football had given more than "help" . . . it was also obvious that the clubs were not opposed to the agency.

At the beginning of November, 1975, FC Amsterdam (whose chairman is an F.A. management committee member!) sold Nico Jansen to Feyenoord for £150,000.

Jansen was driven to Rotterdam to complete the deal by Coster and a Press conference was even held at Inter-Football's offices!

"No!" cried Coster. "We only advised Jansen."

The F.A. stopped the transfer "pending an investigation." Lawyers from all sides became involved and Feyenoord announced they were taking legal proceedings against the F.A. So was Jansen.

One final meeting was held in the offices of the Dutch F.A. in Zeist. The result? Rather startling . . . Jansen was eligible to play for Feyenoord.

And Coster? He resigned from Inter-Football to take up the position as head of the F.A.'s transfer-office.

He is still dealing in players, organising transfers. Not for a percentage any more, just a salary from the F.A.

Romeo Benetti, the AC-Milan hard-man in midfield, is a wine enthusiast.

Here we see him in his cellar with a bottle of vintage Italian wine.

Benetti should play for Italy against England in the World Cup qualifying ties.

Duncan Cummings
'Australia's best-ever-player'

This is Duncan Cummings, at 18 already described as Australia's best-ever player.

Cummings was just 17 when he won his first cap for the Aussies in June, 1975, against China in Melbourne.

Not only did that make him the youngest star to wear the yellow-and-green jersey of Australia . . . but he also scored with his first kick of the game. A record that it is safe to say will never be beaten!

Aged 14, Cummings had a big decision to make. He had proved himself at association football and Australian soccer . . . and he chose the former . . . completely different.

The lad chose soccer . . . soccer as we know it, that is.

Cummings was born in Birmingham, but when he was three his family emigrated to Melbourne.

He has always followed Manchester United and was, in fact, named after the late, great Duncan Edwards, who died in the 1958 Munich air disaster.

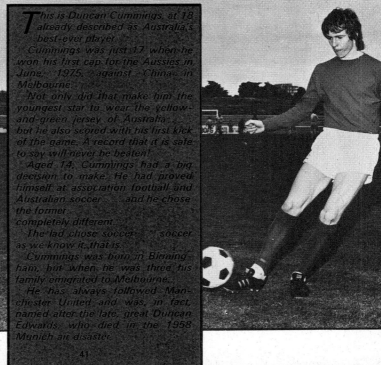

41

JOHAN CRUYFF — GOALKEEPER!

You usually see Holland captain Johan Cruyff SCORING goals. But during training sessions, Johan likes to go between the sticks to show he can SAVE them. Versatility indeed!

PHIL WARMAN
CHARLTON ATHLETIC

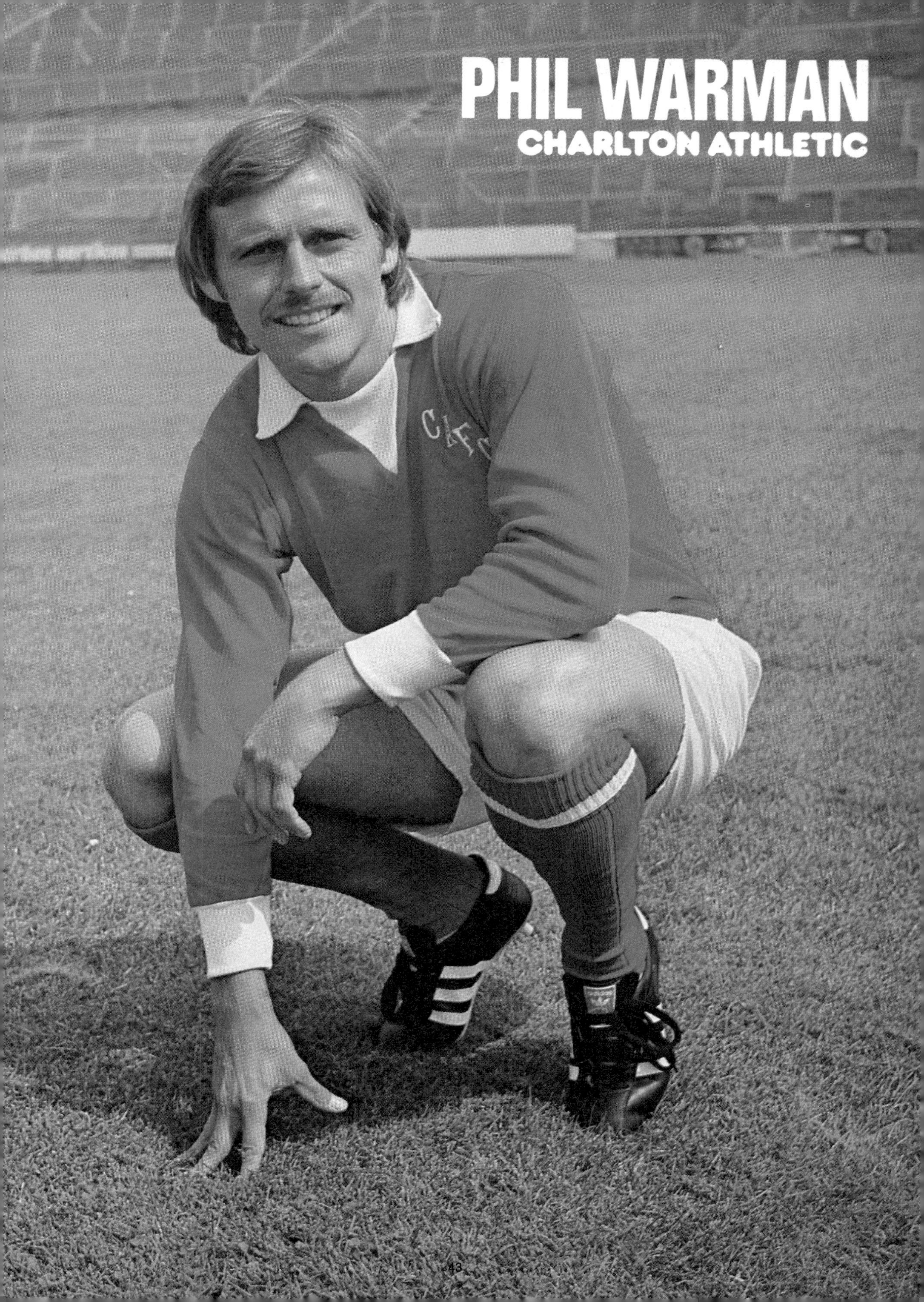

WHEN ASA HARTFORD ALMOST JOINED LEEDS...

Whatever Asa Hartford achieves in his career—and he's achieved quite a lot already—the Manchester City and Scotland midfielder will always be known as the player with a hole in his heart.

It's not a big hole, just the size of a pin-head.

But it was enough to call off the transfer from West Brom to Leeds in November, 1971.

Don Revie was the Leeds manager at the time and he wanted Hartford to strengthen his already impressive Elland Road squad.

Hartford seemed set to be on his way, but the Leeds doctor could not give the final go-ahead because of the heart condition.

"I remember Don Howe, the West Brom manager, calling me into his office," recalls Hartford (how ironic that Howe is now coach at Leeds).

"He told me that he'd received a fabulous offer from Leeds and he was prepared to let me go.

"It was all rather secret and we met Don Revie on the East Lancs Road. The discussions actually took place in his car!

"We agreed terms and all that remained was a routine medical check a couple of days later.

"By then, the newspapers knew all about it. I went to Elland Road on the Friday for the check and to meet my new team-mates.

"The doctor wired me up to one of those machines which took a graph of my heart.

"He took me to see another specialist. By this time I was wondering what was happening.

"The next morning, Don Revie came round my house. He didn't need to say a word. The look on his face said it all.

"Don explained the situation and took me to see yet another heart specialist. More wires and more graphs.

"Eventually, Don had to tell me the worst. There were tears streaming down his face as he left.

"I was very muddled. I think the worst part was switching on my radio as I drove home and hearing the news there.

"I tried to phone my wife to tell her personally, but the line was engaged."

A few days later, Hartford entered a Birmingham Hospital. There WAS a slight hole in his heart but, he was assured, it would not affect his career.

Hartford was told that the condition would correct itself as he got older and there was no reason why he shouldn't continue to play football at the highest level.

His West Brom team-mates welcomed him back with some mickey-taking remarks like: "having a heart-to-heart chat with the boss today, Asa?"

Hartford was soon back in action for West Brom, showing no ill-effects from his recent experience.

In fact, Tommy Docherty, Scotland manager then, awarded him his first full cap against Peru in 1972.

Unfortunately, as West Brom declined, Hartford's relationship soured and in 1974 Manchester City stepped in with a bid of £250,000.

They gave him the usual stringent tests but this time there were no complications.

His form for City and Scotland in the past two years is proof that Asa Hartford has a big heart . . . and there's nothing wrong with it!

...AND MANCHESTER CITY BID FOR STUART PEARSON

Stuart Pearson . . . the new goal-king of Old Trafford, adored by Manchester United's famous Stretford End, not to mention their other thousands of fans.

Stuart Pearson . . . a Red Devil through and through.

Stuart Pearson of Manchester CITY ? Unthinkable—yet this was nearly the case.

The strong-running goal-getter was still a Hull City player, but Terry Neill, their manager at the time, had resigned himself to the fact that he would have to sell his top star.

Ron Saunders, in charge of Manchester City then, agreed terms with Hull—£200,000 was the fee, a tidy sum for 1974.

Unfortunately for Saunders, the deal fell through. City were unable to raise the cash as the proposed transfer of Mike Summerbee to Leeds United had been postponed.

"I was really upset at the time," recalls Pearson.

"The chance to go to a glamour club like Manchester City was something I'd dreamed of. Being so near, yet so far, was very disappointing."

Pearson's dreams of joining a big-name club came true on the eve of the Newcastle United/Liverpool F.A. Cup Final.

"Terry phoned me and told me to come to London. I assumed that a club from the capital had put in an offer for me.

"I was wrong. It was, of course, Manchester United."

Tommy Docherty knew all about Pearson. The Doc had been Neill's number two at Hull for a spell and had always admired the player's skill.

United paid the equivalent of £200,000, which included reserve Peter Fletcher moving to Boothferry Park.

United had just been relegated, yet this did not deter Pearson.

"Let's face it, despite being in Division Two, United were still the biggest club in England. It took me about two seconds to say 'yes' to Tommy Docherty !"

The Reds stayed in the Second Division for the bare minimum of time, winning promotion at the first attempt.

"I shall never forget the run-in to that season. All the hard work and dedication we'd put in was paying off. Fantastic."

Pearson's name was regularly on the goal-sheet and the following season, in Division One, he proved that he was a striker of rare calibre.

Don Revie, the England manager, was impressed by Pearson's style and it came as a surprise to many critics when Pearson began 1976 without a full England cap.

Pearson is set to break a few records in his career . . . but one that he holds—and will surely never be equalled—is when he was sent off for calling a linesman an onion !

This happened during his Hull days in a game against Sheffield Wednesday.

Pearson was on top of the world, having scored twice at Hillsborough, but a linesman's decision at a throw-in incident angered him.

"I just called him an onion. It was more in fun than anything else.

"To my amazement, he called the ref over and I was sent off. I try to keep my mouth shut these days."

45

IAN BRITTON
CHELSEA

BOBBY LENNOX
CELTIC

Stranger than fiction

Have you heard the story about the footballer who signed transfer forms in the House of Commons? Or the one about the Second Division player who turned out for both sides in the same match. You haven't? Well, these are just two of the countless oddities which make soccer such a fascinating game to follow.

Footballers have signed on the dotted line in some strange places. Some have put pen to paper while sitting in the back of cars speeding along motorways, in trains, roadside cafes, night clubs and hotels.

But only one player, Ian Lawther, the former Northern Ireland centre-forward, can say he signed for his new club while at the House of Commons. The transfer took place in 1964 when Lawther moved from Scunthorpe to Brentford for £15,000.

The transfer was arranged by Jack Dunnett, the then chairman of Brentford, who was also M.P. for Nottingham Central. He is now chairman of Notts County.

The story of a player appearing for both sides in the same League match is true, however hard it is to believe. It happened in the 1932-33 season.

Left back Jimmy Oakes turned out for Port Vale in a Second Division match against Charlton at The Valley over Christmas. But thick fog on that Boxing Day led to the match being abandoned.

The fixture was re-arranged for later in the season. But before the rescheduled date, Oakes was transferred to Charlton and he turned out for his new club against his old colleagues in a 2-2 draw.

Manchester United are still recognised as one of the most attractive and best supported clubs in the land.

Record books show that the best crowd they have attracted to Old Trafford was 70,504 for their First Division match with Aston Villa at Christmas in 1920. But in fact, United's record home gate was achieved AWAY from Old Trafford.

A crowd of 82,950 watched them play Arsenal on January 17, 1948, at neighbouring Maine Road. United were still sharing Manchester City's ground while War-damage repairs to Old Trafford were being carried out. The attendance is still a record for an English League match.

Old Trafford has been the famous setting for many important matches attracting large crowds. But it also holds a crowd record which nobody wants to break.

Only 13 people turned up for a League match there in 1921— and that is not a printing error!

The match—between Stockport and Leicester—finished as a goalless draw. The Second Division fixture was switched to Old Trafford because Stockport's ground was closed by the F.A.

If former England skipper, Bobby Moore, ever wants to take up refereeing when his playing days are over, he will have had experience of the big-time behind him. For he became a referee during a First Division match with Wolves at Upton Park in 1970.

Moore had already put West Ham into the lead when he knocked out the referee, Gerrard Lewis, with a headed clearance. Moore acted instinctively and bent over the referee, picked up his whistle and blew to stop play as West Ham built up an attack.

Referee Lewis soon recovered after treatment and re-started play. The fans gave Moore a big round of applause for his sporting action.

Talking of referees, former official Kevin Howley acted promptly when an apple was hurled at him by an irate Everton fan at Goodison Park. Howley picked up the apple, polished it on his shorts, and took a bite before gently rolling it towards the track around the pitch.

The fans liked it and this amusing ritual was repeated many times whenever Howley returned to Merseyside.

"It stopped suddenly," says Howley. "Either the fan ran out of apples or he died, because there were no apples to be seen on my last few visits."

Howley was known throughout his career for his sense of humour, but Mansfield Town were not amused by him in 1962. He booked 10 of the side when they slow-handclapped him off the field after a 2-2 F.A. Cup-tie against Crystal Palace at Selhurst Park.

Almost every season, managers and players protest that the game is being ruined by congested fixture lists. But that situation is nothing new. Just study the matches West Bromwich Albion played back in 1912. In 10 days they played seven games, including an F.A. Cup Final and a replay!

After the Cup defeat, they played four League matches in five days, drawing two and losing the others. It was little wonder that they failed to win any of those seven games.

Hard luck, West Brom!

"My job is to score goals. I don't care how they go in so long as they cross that line. The ball can go in off my behind and I'll be just as happy with that as I would with a rocket shot from 25 yards."

These are the emphatic words of Hearts' glory scorer Drew Busby, the toast of Tynecastle. Busby's entire career has been concerned with making life extremely hectic for 'keepers.

He was one half of the double-act at Airdrie that first put the soccer spotlight on him and Drew Jarvie. They were merchants of menace to defences everywhere and it was only a question of time before they were tempted away from Broomfield.

Jarvie was first to go, joining Aberdeen in a £70,000 deal. There was some talk of Busby joining him at Pittodrie to restore the partnership, but Hearts' former manager Bobby Seith, who left the club three seasons ago, was first in and brought Busby to Tynecastle. The £40,000 transfer fee must be one of the best bargains in soccer dealing.

However, if Seith had had his way several years before that deal Busby probably wouldn't be playing in Scotland today!

When Seith was manager of Preston he hoped to sign Busby from Airdrie. He wanted a courageous front man who could lead the attack, take the knocks and, most important, stick the ball in the net. The deal never went through, Seith finally got his way when Busby later joined him at Tynecastle.

"I was delighted to join Hearts."

says Busby. "There had been plenty of transfer talk, but nothing was happening. It seemed to affect my form at the time.

"I read somewhere that Sunderland were interested. Then someone said Dundee . . . and then Aberdeen. At one point it looked as though every team in Britain were watching me!

"I went out to impress every week. And the harder I tried the worse things seemed to get. Then I heard Hearts were keen on me. I had heard it all before, of course, but I thought this might be genuine.

"Anyway, we were due to play Hearts at Tynecastle around that time and I knew I would have to be at my very best. The funny thing was I don't think I had ever

scored at Tynecastle!

"I just rolled up my sleeves and got on with the game. I tried to put all the transfer talk behind me. Fortunately, I broke my duck and scored the only goal of the game.

"It wasn't long after that when Mr. Seith made Airdrie and myself an offer I couldn't refuse. I was happy with the move and the Hearts fans helped me settle in right away."

The modest Busby doesn't say that he gave the Hearts fans a lot to cheer. He led the line along with Donald Ford, and with these two acting as a spearhead and wingers Kenny Aird and Bobby Prentice sending over a variety of crosses, Hearts soon became one of the most dangerous attacking combinations north of the border.

They had many splendid results —including a 3-0 win against Rangers at Ibrox with Busby scoring two glorious goals. The Hearts fans still talk of one of those games today. Aird stuck a short ball inside the full-back about 20 yards out and went for the one-two with Busby.

Deadly Drew intelligently anticipated Rangers' rearguard action and as they moved to cover Aird he first-timed a magnificent drive high past Peter McCloy for a tremendous goal.

Since John Hagart took over as manager Busby has played a deeper role.

"Mr. Hagart reckons I will get more scoring opportunities by running at defences," says Busby.

Busby—known as "The Buzz" because of the amount of buzzing around he does—is certainly the Ace of Hearts.

All goals the same to 'The Buzz'

score a soccer century

TRANSFERS

Here we've listed players who were transferred during last season. Their former clubs are in brackets. Can you name the clubs they joined? (Award three points for each correct answer).

1. Peter Marinello (Portsmouth) *Motterwell*
2. Bryan Hamilton (Ipswich) *Everton*
3. Phil Boersma (Liverpool) *Middlesborough*
4. Gordon Hill (Millwall) *Man Utd*
5. Brian Alderson (Coventry) *Lstser*
6. Bobby Gould (West Ham—right) *Coyrehones*
7. Tony Young (Man. Utd.) *Acton*
8. John Burridge (Blackpool) *Aston Villa*
9. Willie Young (Aberdeen) *Celtic*
10. Arthur Horsfield (Charlton) *Watford*

MAX. TOTAL	YOUR TOTAL
30	27

ANSWERS

1. Motherwell. 2. Everton. 3. Middlesbrough. 4. Man. Utd. 5. Leicester. 6. Wolves. 7. Charlton. 8. Aston Villa. 9. Tottenham. 10. Watford.

We've wrongly paired some of Britain's League clubs and their grounds. See if you can sort them out. (Award two points for each correct answer).

1. Bootham Crescent (Bristol City) *Sunderland*
2. Elm Park (Partick) *Bury*
3. Rugby Park (York) *Reading*
4. Gigg Lane—below (Sunderland) *Bristol City*
5. Hampden Park (Derby) *Queen's Park*
6. Parkhead (Kilmarnock) *Celtic*
7. Firhill Park (Bury) *Partick*
8. Ashton Gate (Reading) *Partick*
9. Baseball Ground (Celtic) *Kilmarnok*
10. Rokel Park (Queen's Park) *Derby*

MAX. TOTAL	YOUR TOTAL
20	6

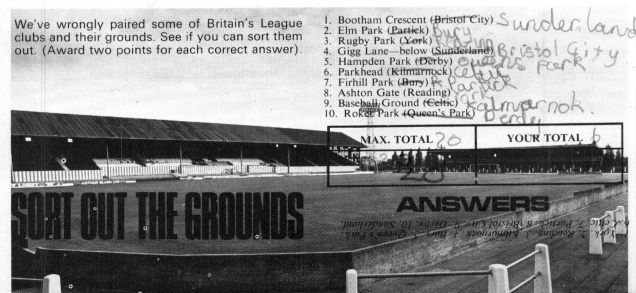

SORT OUT THE GROUNDS

ANSWERS

York. 2. Reading. 3. Kilmarnock. 4. Bury. 5. Queen's Park. 6. Celtic. 7. Partick. 8. Bristol City. 9. Derby. 10. Sunderland.

48

DEFENDERS

(Award one point for each correct answer).

1. Is it correct Keith Newton (Burnley) and Mike England (Cardiff) were both once Blackburn Rovers team-mates?
2. Who played in the number two shirt for West Ham when they won the 1974-75 F.A. Cup Final v. Fulham?
3. How much did Derby pay Sunderland for defender Colin Todd?
4. Man. Utd's Jim Holton was signed from Shrewsbury by Frank O'Farrell or Tommy Docherty?
5. Can you identify the Q.P.R. defender who scored the winning goal for his former club Chelsea in an F.A. Cup Final?
6. Was Emlyn Hughes with Bolton before joining Liverpool?
7. Rangers' John Greig made his full Scotland debut v. England in 1962-63, 1963-64 or 1964-65?
8. Which one of these players isn't a defender—Alan Kennedy (Newcastle), Liam Brady (Arsenal—below), Jeff Blockley (Leicester)?
9. Rearrange the jumbled letters to find the name of a top stopper in the First Division—RNGODO cNUMEQE (SEDEL).
10. True or false: Brighton's Joe Kinnear was a member of Tottenham's 1967 F.A. Cup winning side?

MAX. TOTAL	YOUR TOTAL
10	

ANSWERS

1. Yes. 2. John McDowell. 3. £170,000. 4. Tommy Docherty. 5. David Webb. 6. No—Blackpool. 7. 1963-64. 8. Liam Brady. 9. Gordon McQueen (Leeds). 10. True.

(Award four points for each correct answer).

1. Take a walk along Leeds Road and you'll find the home ground of which club?
2. Which club, formed in 1873, is the oldest in Wales?
3. Derby's Francis Lee has played for two other League clubs —can you name them?
4. Colin Stein (left) was sold to Glasgow Rangers for £80,000 in 1974-75 from which English club?
5. Their home ground is Brockville Park and they are nick-named The Bairns . . . can you identify them?

MAX. TOTAL	YOUR TOTAL
20	0

ANSWERS

1. Huddersfield. 2. Wrexham. 3. Bolton and Manchester City. 4. Coventry City. 5. Falkirk.

LEAGUE CUP

Newcastle United and Manchester City battled their way through to last term's League Cup Final. Below we've listed their opponents Round by Round . . . can you select the correct results? (Award two points for each correct answer).

NEWCASTLE
SECOND: v. Southport (4-0, 5-0, 6-0)
THIRD: v. Bristol Rovers (1-0, 2-0, 3-0)
FOURTH: v. Q.P.R. (2-1, 3-1, 4-1)
QUARTER-FINAL: v. Notts County (1-0, 2-1, 3-2)
SEMI-FINAL: aggregate score v. Spurs (2-1, 3-2, 4-3)
MANCHESTER CITY
SECOND: v. Norwich (4-1, 5-1, or 6-1)
THIRD: v. Nottm. For. (1-0, 2-1, or 3-2)
FOURTH: v. Man. Utd. (2-0, 3-0, or 4-0)
QUARTER-FINALS: v. Mansfield (3-1, 4-2, or 5-3)
SEMI-FINALS: aggregate score v. Middlesbrough (2-1, 3-1, or 4-1)

MAX. TOTAL	YOUR TOTAL
20	

ANSWERS

NEWCASTLE. SECOND: 6-0. THIRD: 2-0. FOURTH: 3-1. Q.F.: 1-0. SEMI: 3-2 (on aggregate). MANCHESTER CITY. SECOND: 6-1. THIRD: 2-1. FOURTH: 4-0. Q.F.: 4-2. SEMI: 4-1 (on aggregate). MANCHESTER CITY. SECOND: 6-1 (City's Dennis Tueart is shown scoring from a penalty in the second replay). THIRD: 2-1. FOURTH: 4-0. Q.F.: 4-2. SEMI: 4-1 (on aggregate).

Somebody once asked me what I do with all the spare time I have between training sessions and watching the team play on a Saturday.

Unfortunately, I did not have the time to answer! Because soccer management is a "24 hours-a-day" operation, and managers simply do not have the lengthy gaps people imagine.

There are two faces of management. There's the face everybody knows, where the manager selects the side, conducts transfers, solves injury problems and deals with training.

But the period between is crammed with activity. That's the lesser-known face. The scouting, travelling, public functions, public relations and endless administrative duties punctuated by sleep and brief spells of relaxation with your family.

Football management has now reached saturation point. It's the quart-in-the-pint-pot story. Only the growth of the game, and the inflation problems affecting it, add to the pressure.

Of course the whole syndrome points to one thing, and that's a successful team playing in a good-looking stadium. That's the ultimate aim. Everything you do is geared to that target.

Ironically, it's when everything is running smoothly that you get those longed-for moments of peace and quiet. The hard work must be put in day after day until success is achieved. And then, after a brief spell of feeling satisfied, you have to work just as hard to ensure your success continues.

Anyone can write eleven names on a team-sheet. The problem is

THE TWO FACES OF MANAGEMENT

The fine new grandstand at Craven Cottage, built at a cost of around £250,000, and with a capacity of 5,000.

by ALEC STOCK, Fulham

writing down eleven names you know will comprise a team. That's a lot tougher than many people imagine.

The balance must be right. The mood must be right when they take the field. A manager's only tools are words. And then there's a limit to how many different things you can say. But if the mood is right, the battle's half-won. That responsibility rests with the manager.

Team-Building

So the week's last training session is over, the team for Saturday is pinned on the wall and the manager's door is firmly shut. What goes on in there when it appears there's nothing else to do?

On that question hangs the whole crux of the job. Football is all about team-building. It's all about today. Yesterday is history, and tomorrow will be just fine if things are done properly today.

You sit at your desk staring at four walls, but your mind is constantly on the problem of team-building.

Some clubs have the cash to go out and buy a player, others have favourable situations when it comes to the crunch. They may have just the right lad for a part-exchange deal.

You cut your cloth accordingly. At Fulham we have to build our own side . . . from scratch. That means going to see schoolboy games, youth games, reserve games—never knowing when you'll come across a good prospect.

It can be frustrating. It can be worrying. But it must be done if that constant flow is to be maintained through the club ranks. And it's that team-building headache that stays with you while you're driving home after a 14-hour day, or even when you're taking your family out to dinner.

You would be surprised just how much work is crammed into a manager's week.

A typical week started for me with training in the morning, a chat to the players, a check on weekend injury problems and the usual telephone conversations with the Press. In the afternoon I dashed off to pick up a film of our F.A. Cup Final with West Ham, came back to collect the players and go off on another trip to where the film was to be shown.

Mr. Stock has tremendous regard for Alan Mullery, Footballer of the Year in 1975.

By the time I'd wrapped up Monday, I was crawling home in thick fog and finally got to bed at 12.45.

Tuesday morning, training again before dashing off to watch the reserves playing. Important, this, with three players coming back following spells out through injury. Home by midnight.

Wednesday started with a host of phone calls and queries and a lunch appointment.

Two interviews in the afternoon meant I was too late to take in a reserve game I'd hoped to see. I felt I'd cheated by missing that match.

Thursday's training session and usual office work were followed by a talk to the Guildford Referees in the evening and another late night.

Friday, hectic as always. Team selection, last-minute problems ironed out, public relations and Press work at its busiest and a 7.30 dinner appointment (business, of course).

Saturday started at 8 a.m., when I collected a club director and drove to Kings Cross to set out for our game. Another 13-hour day.

That, as an average weekly schedule over ten months, can be —and is—shattering.

The public relations side of the job is very important. I want football to have the image it deserves, and I want Fulham to maintain the image they are proud of. Taking just that side of the job alone represents hours of work.

I love football, I love the job. But if there's one thing that makes me want to cry it's to see standards slipping. It takes only a handful of players to be in the headlines for the wrong reasons to give footballers in general a bad image.

In my football career I've found professional footballers a great bunch. And they are the first to comment and show anger and resentment when one of their own ranks lets the side down, either appearance-wise or by saying all the controversial things guaranteed to bring the spotlight on them.

Players have pride in themselves and in their club. More important they *want* to have pride. But just one bad apple can upset the whole cart. Here, a manager has to be so careful to ensure the club as a whole stays happy. You cannot risk a wrong influence.

Football spins by public opinion and the public expect certain standards. They are entitled to. I set out to maintain those standards. At Fulham, our standards are second to none. But then, with men of the calibre of Alan Mullery and Bobby Moore in the side, we were fortunate.

I expect both to enter management. And they will succeed. But I give them, and any young man about to embark on a managerial career, the following advice:

You must have the capacity to stick with it. Take the ups and downs as they come and keep striving for the best, for the top. The first thing to hit you will be the feeling of utter frustration when match-day arrives. All that work during the week aimed at 90 minutes of make or break. That's when it comes to the crunch . . . when you are helpless. Sitting up in the stand or on the bench, you might as well go for a walk for all the use you are to the team while they are playing.

That's what makes the job so fascinating, and at times, so intangible. How do you measure effort? Not with a thermometer. How do you gauge complete athletic fitness? If you win 4–0 you feel great. But if you lose 1–0, does that mean you were not properly fit?

It's all about learning to assess individuals, bringing the best out of eleven different young men.

Suddenly it's Monday morning again, the phones are ringing and you have to convince everyone that, despite Saturday's defeat, this is going to be a wonderful week . . . if you have the time.

Mr. Stock did wonders in steering Fulham to the F.A. Cup Final in 1975. Unfortunately they lost 2-0 to fellow Londoners, West Ham.

Peter's great comeback

Four years ago Peter Thompson was told by a medical specialist: "You've only 12 months left in the game."

That terse but chilling statement came following the removal of two cartilages from his left knee.

With the 1976/77 season in full swing, the ex-wing wonder of Liverpool is still defying that specialist as he dribbles, feints, and darts down the left flank for Bolton Wanderers.

"Had my contract with Liverpool run out at the end of the 1972/73 season I would have retired," admits Peter.

"I felt awful. I wasn't wanted. I'd play a few games in the reserves but I was just going through the motions.

"I'd been ten years at the top, with a top club . . . Liverpool.

"Steve Heighway had taken over my spot in the first-team and I was convinced no other club would want me because I'd never pass a medical."

Then, like manna from heaven, an offer came to take Peter on a four-week loan. The club in question was Second Division Bolton Wanderers, six months after they'd clinched the Championship of Division Three.

The ex-Kop idol's reaction was to immediately grab at his new-found life-line and vow to tear

Second Division defences apart.

"Things didn't quite turn out that way," reflected Peter. "I'd lost some of my pace. Playing before half-empty terraces didn't

inspire me then, either. There was an obvious lack of atmosphere.

"But I received some encouraging news. I went to see a specialist in Manchester—that was in the last few weeks of 1973—and he confidently predicted I'd get two or three more seasons out of the game.

"Psychologically, it was the best boost I could have had. My form improved no end and I established myself as a regular member of the first-team during the second half of the 1973/74 season.

"I'm 34, and now in my fourth season with Bolton, and have suffered no further knee trouble."

The cost to Bolton was a bargain £20,000.

"Shanks—Bill Shankly, my manager at Liverpool—never tried to make me change my style—of a traditional winger.

"When I came to Bolton Jimmy Armfield was in charge. He never wanted me to alter my ways. And neither has our present boss, Ian Greaves."

Peter then talked of his future plans, one of which won't please the Burnden Park faithful.

"I plan to retire at the end of this season and have no intentions of staying in the game.

"My decision stems back to the time I was told I was finished in football. I bought a caravan site at a place called Knott End, near Blackpool.

"I've since bought another two-and-half acres for the same purpose and in all there are over 100 caravans situated on my sites.

"In any case, I knew one day it would all come to an end. So I was determined to obtain something that would enable my wife, myself, and our children to continue to live a life we've been accustomed to."

Peter's retirement to his caravan sites will leave the footballing folk in Liverpool and Bolton breathing a sigh of sadness.

But out there on the park they'll always remember him as a sight worth seeing.

Greatest players I've ever seen

by JEFF BLOCKLEY, Leicester

Jeff Blockley, the Leicester defender, includes players from abroad as well as from Britain in his list of all-time greats, starting with the man he rates as the complete back-four player—Franz Beckenbauer.

"Beckenbauer's ability to remain cool in every situation, to be in control, makes him an outstanding player, and captain," says Jeff. "He does not become rattled under pressure, as some defenders do.

"He is good to watch from the stand, but is even more impressive when you meet him on the field, as I have. Playing against him, you notice at close range the qualities that have made him famous.

"To begin with, he never seems to lack the pace to cover up quickly when his defence is in trouble—this comes from possessing a quick soccer brain, and Beckenbauer's thinking is often a split-second ahead of most other players.

"Then there is his ball control—he can change a desperate defensive situation for his side into one which puts them on the attack by making an intelligent pass. No wild clearances for him.

"And for me, Beckenbauer was every bit as effective as a midfield man, before moving into the back-four. He was never afraid to take on a man or two when trying to open up the opposing defence, and always showed perfect balance when running with the ball.

"Add everything else to his powers of leadership, and you find that he lacks nothing in his soccer make-up. His influence on his colleagues in the West German side during the last World Cup were tremendous."

Not to be left out of Blockley's selection of great players is the idol of Brazil, Pele—another whom Jeff believes is well equipped in every way for his role as a soccer super-man.

"Pele has remarkable vision, the gift of seeing the ball more clearly than most and also judging every situation accurately, whether the play is near him or in a different part of the field.

"And he is a power player, able to accelerate quickly and carve a way through any defence—this strength is linked up with a control of the ball at speed which is remarkable.

"I think that everybody who has seen Pele play is so familiar with his abilities that it seems unnecessary to list them. Such a player comes only once in a lifetime.

"I once saw him in an exhibition match and he was superb.

Another player who Jeff rates as World-class is George Best—and he speaks with knowledge gained from playing against the ex-Manchester United star.

"When George was in his hey-day, defences were unable to hold him. Plans could be laid, and extra men detailed to watch him—but it was all useless if Best was on form.

"He had pace and a swerve that could take anybody the wrong way—just when you thought you had George cornered he would be off in another direction. At his peak, Best could be as good as Pele, because he had a variety of tricks.

"In Russia, there is a player called Oleg Blochin who I think will earn himself a reputation as a great forward. For the past three seasons he has been his country's top scorer, and this season he looks like topping the scoring charts again for Dynamo Kiev.

"I have seen him on television and he seems to have all the assets that make players world famous."

"OLEG BLOCHIN — Russia's top scorer"

Greatest players I've ever seen

by BRYAN ROBSON, Sunderland

As a man with a well-earned reputation for scoring goals, it is not surprising that Sunderland's Bryan Robson includes former ace-marksman Jimmy Greaves as the first of a quintette of all-time great players.

"Greaves was a tremendous opportunist," says Bryan. "His coolness in the penalty area was one of his greatest assets, and there was never any danger of him missing a goal because of over-excitement at a critical moment.

"But he had so many things in his favour—Jimmy's control of the ball was superb at all times, he was quick-moving with uncanny balance, and very good at splitting a defence with deadly accurate passes.

"He could ghost his way past opposing players, and defenders who tried to nail him often found they had connected only with thin air.

"Nothing seemed to perturb Greaves, and I have seen him score goals in all sorts of ways—by solo dashes, close-range efforts and also by kidding the goalkeeper to move the wrong way.

"Everything that Jimmy did had class and flair, and he relied on skill alone against defenders who were physically bigger and stronger than himself. Summing up, he had everything."

For his No. 1 defender Robson selects one of England's great captains, Bobby Moore, who was a club-mate of Bryan's in his West Ham days.

Robson says: "Bobby made everything he did look so easy—and this was entirely due to the way he could read a game. His positional play was so good that he rarely seemed to be extended, and gave the impression of being completely unflappable.

"But he is much more than a purely defensive player or spoiler—his distribution is immaculate and he starts many attacks.

"And nothing seems to get on top of him. The bigger the occasion, the more tense the atmosphere is in the dressing room among the other players, the cooler Bobby becomes.

"This is one of the reasons he is world-class. He is essentially a big-game player.

"Among back-four men, he was in a class of his own during his career at Upton Park."

Three ex-Manchester United stars figure among Bryan's selection of great players, and it is a trio calculated to cause panic in any defence—George Best, Denis Law and Bobby Charlton.

"Best in his hey-day would have earned his place in any forward line in the world—he never hesitated to take on two or three players at a time when he set off on one of his dribbles. His zest for the game, and his footwork, were really brilliant, and in addition he was brave enough never to be put off by hard tackling.

"Neither was Law, a terrific crowd-pleaser who was an entertainer as well as an outstanding player. His confidence, his razor-sharp football brain and sharpness in the opposing penalty area made him dangerous at any stage of a match.

"About Bobby Charlton—what can I say that has not already been said? His explosive shooting, plus speed and power on the ball when moving forward were guaranteed to set the crowds roaring.

"He could never be kept out the headlines yet in spite of his fame remained level-headed and a credit to the game.

"Lastly, if I had to name another player I consider great, it would be Geoff Hurst. In today's soccer he could be described as the perfect target man—good in the air, he can upset any defence."

Greatest players I've ever seen

by GEOFF NULTY, Newcastle

Newcastle United skipper Geoff Nulty has no doubts in his mind when it comes to naming the star who stands out even in the company of great players—he cites Pele, ex-Brazil and now of New York Cosmos, as the man who has all the talents.

"Pele is fantastic," says Nulty. "Ball control, heading ability, shooting, reading the game, passing and tackling are all things he excels in—he has no weaknesses.

"On top of this, he is very strong, which is the reason he can stand up to rough treatment so well. For many years he has been a heavily-marked man with defenders in his own country and all over the world doing all they can to stop him—but he has still delivered the goods.

"And one of his most remarkable assets is one which is usually not mentioned—the ability to tackle. Many forwards are weak in this department, but Pele can really fight for the ball.

"He is also what I would describe as a conscientious player—he always works at turning in as good a performance as possible and never seems to rest on his laurels."

Having selected Pele as top of his great player list, Geoff nominates George Best as the No. 2 choice.

"To take the sort of stick that George took over the years meant having a lot of courage—obviously, Best had this and combined it with his skill to become a great attacking player.

"But I believe that he was so unique that he could have also moulded himself into a first-class defender. He could tackle like a tiger, which meant that if he did lose the ball he went all out to win it back.

"And he was a great crowd-puller. As a rule, forwards figure more in the headlines than defenders because of the nature of their game, but when George was on form he captured all the limelight for himself.

"Today he is trying to make a come back, and establish himself again. But some of my strongest memories of Best are in the period up to 1970, when forwards received less protection than they do now, and when he took plenty of punishment and still led defenders a dance."

While Nulty is sure that it is next to impossible to find forwards to overshadow Pele and Best, he is equally certain that there has not been a better goalkeeper in soccer history than Gordon Banks.

"I was lucky enough to be at Bolton when Gordon was there, and wonder if there has ever been a goalkeeper with his judgement.

"In the air, cutting out crosses and stuff like that, and in dealing with shots on the floor, Banks was superb. And where will you ever see a better save than the one he made from Pele's header in the World Cup?

"I still treasure a photograph I had taken with Banks—he was a true professional, always looking for improvement, even with his great gifts.

"Oddly enough, there was one player who I list as a World-class defender who was considered by some to have several defects in his game—this was Bobby Moore. There was talk that his tackling and headwork were poor, he was slow and a bad passer of the ball—yet he was outstanding for England!

And lastly, I feel I must mention Jimmy Greaves. At the art of goal-scoring his ability to slot the ball into the net from any angle was remarkable—and scoring is what the game is all about.

Greatest players I've ever seen

by MICKEY WALSH, Blackpool

The dazzling skills of Pele put him head and shoulders above any of the other great names in soccer, according to Blackpool's Mickey Walsh.

"No other player can measure up to Pele for all-round ability and the impact he can have on a game—he can slow it down, play it at his own pace, suddenly switch the attack from one point to another and always keeps the opposing defence at full stretch.

"Pele is also a master at finding the weakest links in a defence and then putting on the pressure. And he weighs his passes perfectly, so that his team-mates can get the fullest advantage out of them.

"Along with the skill in his feet, he has the perfect temperament. Many class ball-players are inconsistent or can be goaded by hard tackling, but not Pele. I'm not saying he can't lose his temper, but he does control it better than most players who come in for close marking.

"And this means it is very difficult to hustle him out of his stride, especially when his uncanny positional sense enables him to find space where nobody else could."

Having placed Pele in a class of his own, Mickey believes that George Best at his peak comes next to the immortal Brazilian for pure football ability.

Walsh says: "George was an individualist who also worked for the benefit of the whole team. He could make goals as well as score them, and do it in a variety of ways.

"He was deadly around the six-yard line, twisting like an eel to screw the ball past the goalkeeper. Or I have seen him set off from the half-way mark, taking on and beating three or four players before scoring.

"And Best has been one of those players with an air about them that draws the spectators through the turnstiles in thousands. I always think forwards can do this better than defenders, because their business is to score goals.

"But George did more than simply putting the ball in the net, or creating chances for others—it was the way he did it, with style and dash, that made him such a great attraction.

"About scoring goals—nobody does this any better than Gerd Muller, of West Germany. Here is a forward who lacks the talent of Pele or Best, but has a genius for making the most of chances inside the penalty area.

"By his flair for finishing, Muller gets my vote as a soccer great. His determination and positional sense make him a real headache to defences, and he has proved this at club and international level.

"Outside the box, Muller is not an exceptional player—he is not in the habit of hitting in goals from long range or indulging in solo runs.

"But at close range he has an incredible ability to turn quickly in a very limited space and get in his shot before being tackled, and this gift is one of the main reasons for his success. The others are courage and big-match temperament."

Mickey's fourth choice in the select few he nominates as the best he has seen is Johan Cruyff, who the Blackpool player thinks resembles George Best in some aspects of his game.

"Cruyff's change of pace when running with the ball and his balance remind me of Best, also his confidence. And Cruyff has the poise of a man who knows he is capable of challenging the best of defenders and coming out on top.

"He can shield the ball well, too, which makes it awkward to dispossess him, plus a body swerve that helps to keep him out of trouble."

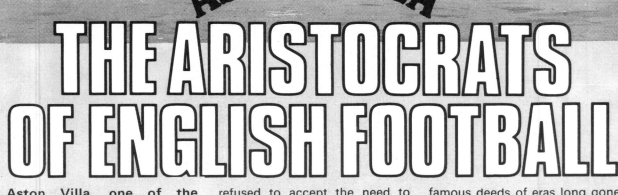

THE ARISTOCRATS OF ENGLISH FOOTBALL

Aston Villa, one of the greatest names in soccer, have won more honours than any other club in the Football League.

Six times League Champions . . . seven F.A. Cup successes . . . two League Cup triumphs . . . Second and Third Division titles . . . and a League and F.A. Cup double, a feat only equalled by Preston, Spurs and Arsenal.

Few clubs have had such a long and honoured history, nor one which has been so turbulent and traumatic.

Tradition and the search for former glories was for many years too heavy a burden for the club. In recent decades Villa suffered because the boardroom powers refused to accept the need to change and go forward with the times.

The ghost of Villa past haunted the vast museum-like red-brick stadium. Portraits of bewhiskered players in long shorts, ankle-length boots and laced-up shirts looked down from the corridor walls, reminding everyone of famous deeds of eras long gone . . . eras many thought best forgotten.

Disappointment after disappointment ended in disaster in 1970 after the club had plunged from the First to the Third Division in just three short, highly-controversial years.

But with the coming of man-

Bayliss (West Brom) heads for goal during the 1887 F.A. Cup which Villa won 2-0 at the Oval.

The team which won the Double in 1896-97.

ager Ron Saunders in 1974, history was just a subject for the record books. The past was last Saturday's game.

The new Aston Villa emerged . . . a team capable of facing the future and of reaching at least some of the gold standards achieved a life-time ago.

Aston Villa was born in humble surroundings . . . underneath a lamp-post in Handsworth one evening in March, 1874.

Four members of Aston Villa Cricket Club thought the odd game of football would be a good way of keeping fit throughout the winter months.

One of the four, C. H. Midgeley, was appointed secretary and he collected a shilling from the other three and agreed to form a football team.

Twelve members of the Villa Cross Wesleyan Chapel in Aston were recruited and a match was arranged against St. Mary's, Aston Brook . . . a rugby club!

After some aguments the match was played 15-a-side under rugby rules in the first-half and as a conventional soccer match in the second. Villa won 1–0.

Two years later, as the team assembled at Aston Park to play a friendly, they found they were one man short.

A young clerk named George Ramsey just happened to be walking past and asked if he could make up the number.

He played so well he was appointed captain of the club and was eventually to serve as skipper, secretary and vice-president for 59 years.

In 1887, two years after professionalism had been legalised, Aston Villa won the F.A. Cup for the first time, beating West Bromwich Albion 2–0 in the Final at Kennington Oval.

The following year they

became one of the 12 pioneer members of the newly-formed Football League, and were a truly dominant force for many seasons after.

In one fantastic spell between 1892 and 1905, they captured the First Division title five times and reached four F.A. Cup Finals, winning three of them.

Those glory years were highlighted in 1896–97 when Villa won the coveted Double, the last time it was to be achieved for 64 years.

That wonderful season they finished 11 points clear of runners-up Sheffield United, losing just four of their 30 League matches.

Eric Houghton, the goal-ace who became manager

In the Cup, Villa beat Everton 3–2 in a Final still described by soccer historians as an all-time classic.

So Aston Villa had won the Cup for the third time, but it was a new trophy they carried back to the Midlands.

In 1895, shortly after they had beaten West Brom 1–0 in the Final, the Cup was stolen while on display in a local shop window and was never recovered.

The Double-winning side contained eight internationals, among them skipper John Devey, Jimmy Crabtree, "Gentle" Howard Spencer and James Cowan.

Towards the end of that historic campaign, on 17th April, 1897, the club played their first match at Villa Park, defeating Blackburn Rovers 3–0. There was no doubt it was the finest soccer stadium in the country—a far cry from their humble Wellington Road ground at Perry Bar.

In their first three seasons at Villa Park, the side only lost three games as they went on to win the Championship twice more, in 1898–99 and 1899–1900.

Five years later, Villa won the Cup again after beating Newcastle United at Crystal Palace, thanks to two great goals by Harry Hampton, signed from Wellington Town in 1904.

A real favourite with the Villa Park fans, 'Appy 'Arry 'Ampton went on to score 213 League goals for the club, a record unbeaten even today. What would 'Appy 'Arry be worth on present values?

With the aid of Hampton's goal-power, Villa were Champions again in 1910, runners-up no less than five times in 13 seasons and won the F.A. Cup for the fifth time in 1913 when they beat Sunderland 1–0 in the Final at Crystal Palace.

When soccer resumed after the First World War, in 1919–20, Villa ended the term ninth in the First Division with 42 points from 42 games . . . 18 behind the Champions West Bromwich Albion.

But the club did find success in the Cup Final at Stamford Bridge, when a goal from Billy Kirton was enough to win the trophy.

Kirton wasn't the only Villa hero of those times, though, the team contained a host of big-named stars . . . players who were household names throughout the country.

There was goalkeeper Sam Hardy, skipper Billy Walker who went on to equal Harry Hampton's League goals record, and centre-half Frank Barson, one of the most suspended players in the history of the game.

Aston Villa celebrated their Jubilee Year in 1924 by reaching the second F.A. Cup Final to be held at Wembley Stadium.

With a side listing five of the 1920 Cup-winners, Villa were beaten 2–0 by Newcastle United. Sadly, that was to be the club's last chance to win more silverware for 33 years!

In 1925 they finished 15th in the First Division, but for the next five seasons their League positions were: sixth, tenth, eighth, third and fourth. Not an unimpressive record for other clubs, but a poor one for a club as proud as Aston Villa.

Then in 1930-31 they ended as Championship runners-up to Arsenal with a total of 59 points, seven behind the leaders. But no club in the Football League scored more goals that season. Villa totalled 128, one more than Arsenal and 26 more than third-placed Sheffield Wednesday.

Of that huge tally, Tom "Pongo" Waring hit 49 and Eric Houghton 30. In a fine career that spanned 20 years at Villa Park, Houghton was to score 200 goals, many from penalties and free-kicks.

Eric later returned to the club, and steered them to their first major honour since 1920 when they won the F.A. Cup in 1957.

At the end of the 1932–33 season, Villa were again runners-up to Champions Arsenal, three points above third-placed Sheffield Wednesday—the same order as 1931.

Just as this was the start of an exciting new era for The Gunners, it was the beginning of the great decline, for once high-and-mighty Villa.

In 1935, Arsenal were again Champions, and Villa lay 12 places below them. With the slide came the appointment of the club's first team-manager Jimmy McMullan, the former Manchester City and Scotland captain.

Unfortunately, McMullan's experience couldn't stop Villa making a sensational dive into the Second Division along with Blackburn Rovers the following season, in 1935–36.

McMullan was replaced by Jimmy Hogan and two years later the club won the Second Division Championship, four points clear of runners-up Manchester United.

Not only did Hogan bring discipline to the side, but also a much-needed determination and sense of pride. Among the players responsible for the club's climb back to the big-time were Scottish international Alex Massie, England's Frank Broome and Mr. Goals himself, Eric Houghton. That same term, Villa reached the F.A. Cup Semi-Final and the

Above: Peter McParland (not in picture) got two goals for Villa against Man. Utd. in the 1957 F.A. Cup Final. Left: One of the club's heroes of the 1920s, Frank Barson.

players and fans had every reason to believe they were heading for more success. But then came World War Two.

When hostilities ceased, the fans swarmed back to Villa Park expecting the club to carry on where they left off. Unhappily, the expected triumphs didn't come.

The directors didn't make the necessary changes to bring the club into line with post-War methods and ideas.

Alex Massie was appointed manager but could do little to inject life into the team, and by January 1949 they found themselves firmly planted at the bottom of the First Division with just 16 points from 23 games.

Money was spent, around £50,000, on new players and for the rest of the 1948–49 season the side performed a minor miracle to finish tenth.

Instead of building on that surge of new-found confidence, the boardroom again sat back watching other clubs such as

Sunderland, Tottenham Hotspur, Wolverhampton Wanderers and Newcastle United, make progress. Villa were being left behind.

Alex Massie left just before the start of the 1950–51 campaign. Disillusioned players also went. Great stars such as Welsh international centre-forward Trevor Ford, Tommy Thompson and Danny Blanchflower, who was sold to Spurs for £30,000.

Many older Villa fans will tell you that the decision to sell the stylish Northern Ireland wing-half was one of the club's biggest errors of judgment. Who can say he wouldn't have led Villa to the same triumphs as he did Spurs, a club destined to equal Villa's Double-winning feat.

Massie was replaced by George Martin, who in turn was sacked. Former Villa hero Eric Houghton finally took over in September, 1953, after finding success at Notts County.

Under Houghton's calm guidance, Villa won the F.A. Cup for the seventh record-breaking time in 1957, by beating Manchester United 2–1 at Wembley.

To everyone outside Villa Park it was a hollow victory against a side already hailed as League Champions. Most people expected the Red Devils to win and so become the first club since Villa to clinch the Double.

Peter McParland, the Northern Ireland winger, scored both Villa goals after colliding with and injuring United's 'keeper Ray Wood.

Despite a brave and spirited come-back, weakened United failed to shake a firm, resolute Villa side determined to bring the

Cup back to the Midlands.

So Villa won, with the nucleus of a team looking strong enough to go on to further honours.

Apart from McParland, there was 'keeper Nigel Sims, Stan Lynn, Stan Crowther, Jimmy Dugdale, Jackie Sewell, Pat Saward and Johnny Dixon.

However, as in previous years, nothing but disappointment and struggle followed.

In 1957–58 they were beaten in the Third Round of the F.A. Cup by the then Second Division Stoke City and ended the term 14th in Division One.

Still the club were reluctant to progress and face the 1960s. They refused to join forces temporarily with neighbouring Birmingham

Vic Crowe, manager from 1971-74.

City to field a side to compete in the European Fairs Cup . . . failed to recognise the need for flood-lights . . . or adopt a youth policy to provide Villa with future stars.

Christmas 1958 brought no presents to manager Houghton. He was replaced by Joe Mercer, the former Everton, Arsenal and England skipper, who arrived from Sheffield United.

Despite Joe's influence and experience and the goal-power of a young up-and-coming centre-forward named Gerry Hitchens, Aston Villa were rele-gated at the end of the season.

A year later they were back as Second Division Champions, one point above Cardiff City and nine more than third placed Liverpool. That same season Villa also reached the F.A. Cup Semi-Finals, only to lose 1–0 to League title runners-up Wolves.

Also that term Peter McParland scored 22 goals in the League, while Gerry Hitchens—later to win England caps before moving to Inter-Milan for £85,000—grabbed six in a 11–1 thrashing of Charlton Athletic.

Alongside McParland and Hitchens, Joe Mercer had brought in Harry Burrows, John Sleeuwenhoek, Alan Deakin, young Charlie Aitken, and an exciting forward from Blackburn Rovers, Derek Dougan.

Welsh international Phil Woosnam came from West Ham to add craft and flair to the mid-field . . . but apart from brief flashes of brilliance the team began to slip.

They did win the very first League Cup in 1961, when they defeated Rotherham over two-legs, but at the time the tourna-ment was regarded as second-rate . . . a consolation prize for the lower clubs.

Gradually, Villa fell away, so

December, 1968, and Tommy Docherty is welcomed by the new board of directors.

did the fans. Joe Mercer's health suffered and in July, 1964, his contract was cancelled by mutual consent.

Dick Taylor took over and reigned for three years until he was sacked in May, 1967, after the club had been relegated along with Blackpool.

Really, though, Taylor had been given little chance to achieve success. Practically no money had been made available for new players and several deals had fallen through because Villa wouldn't pay wages comparable with other First Division clubs.

The day he left Villa Park, Dick Taylor gave the club directors this warning: "You must get around and find out more about what's going on at other clubs before it's too late."

Tommy Cummings was handed the unenviable task of taking the club back to the First Division. But 16 months later and with Villa at the bottom of Division Two, he and coach Malcolm Musgrove were dismissed.

There seemed nothing left for one-proud Aston Villa. In debt with fast-dwindling crowds, a dispirited team and little hope of League salvation. Some whis-pered they might even go out of existence if they dropped down into Division Three.

Finally, in December, 1968, after a great deal of pressure from shareholders, a £750,000 take-over bid lead by a financier named Pat Matthews and a desperate behind-the-scenes "revolution", the old board of directors were forced to resign.

A few days later, with Midland businessman Doug Ellis heading a new regime, Tommy Docherty—after a brief encounter at Q.P.R. — bravely accepted the challenge of taking the now run-down Aston Villa back to the heights.

Even a massive blood-trans-fusion of £275,000 on new players, including new skipper Brian Tiler from Rotherham, one of Docherty's former clubs, came too late; the slide had been left

Ron Saunders and Ian Ross after League Cup triumph.

Veteran defender Charlie Aitken.

unchecked far too long.

Not surprisingly, The Doc failed to cure his ailing patient and midway through the 1969-70 season, after 13 stormy, controversial months, was sacked.

The club's former Welsh international star Vic Crowe succeeded Docherty, but couldn't save them from being relegated to the Third Division, along with Preston, another fallen giant of the past.

Villa kicked-off their Third Division career with a 3—2 home win against Chesterfield, watched by a crowd of nearly 17,000. At least the fantastic upsurge of enthusiasm and support created by Docherty had not deserted them.

With players such as John Dunn, Brian Tiler, Fred Turnbull, Charlie Aitken, Pat McMahon (from Celtic), Bruce Rioch (from Luton), Ian "Chico" Hamilton (from Southend) and Andy Lochhead (from Leicester), Villa settled down well in unfamiliar surroundings. They were involved in the promotion race all season and reached the League Cup Final.

Despite a tremendous performance against First Division giant, Spurs, they lost 2—0. But out of defeat came a pride and

confidence which helped to get them out of the Third Division the following term, 1971—72.

"Our aim is to regain our First Division status for 1974—the club's centenary year," said manager Crowe at the start of the 1972—73 season.

For a while it seemed Villa would win promotion from Division Two, but in the end they were beaten into third place by leaders Burnley and Q.P.R. Despite that disappointment, it was clear to all . . . Aston Villa were a force to be reckoned with . . . they were the talk of the country . . . THEY WERE ON THEIR WAY BACK!

Jim Cumbes had replaced Dunn in goal. Charlie Aitken was as solid and dependable as ever. Ian Ross arrived from Liverpool, John Robson from Derby, Ray Graydon from Bristol Rovers. Youngsters such as Brian Little and Keith Leonard were establishing themselves as stars of the future.

Fans responded even more to the new Villa and a crowd of 40,000 saw a tense promotion battle against Burnley at Villa Park in early January, 1973.

Attendance records had been broken in the Third Division and players bought for fees previously thought impossible in that sphere. Now in Division Two, gates at Villa Park were looked upon with envy by many of the First Division giants. Only Manchester United could match the passion of their fans.

In spite of all the following and headlines, could the team make good Vic Crowe's promise and get back into the First Division in 1974?

No—a slump saw Villa end 1973—74 a disastrous ninth from bottom.

A few weeks later, Crowe and his assistant Ron Wylie paid the price of failure and were sacked.

Then, on June 4th, 1974, after much speculation as to Crowe's successor, Ron Saunders, dismissed by Manchester City after just five months at Maine Road, was appointed the new manager.

Quietly, without fuss, Mr. Saunders set about realising his first objective—promotion back to the First Division where Aston Villa undoubtedly belonged.

He bought two players, both midfielders, Frank Carrodus from Manchester City and Leighton Phillips from Cardiff — for £100,000 each.

Under Ron Saunders' leadership, Villa not only swept to promotion as runners-up to Manchester United, but they beat Norwich City 1—0 at Wembley to win the Lague Cup for the second time.

Cup-winner for Villa that day was Ray Graydon, who topped Division Two with 27 League and Cup goals.

Villa were easily the most successful side in the country from January, 1975, to the end of the 1974—75 term.

The team dropped a mere four points from their last 18 League matches and scored a tremendous 28 goals while winning eight away games. That's entertainment.

After Villa's most successful season in over 30 years, Ron Saunders was deservedly voted "Manager of the Year".

The Villa boss wasn't content to sit back and rest on his achievements.

He spent £210,000 to sign 'keeper John Burridge from Blackpool and Andy Gray, a dashing Scottish Under-23 goal-scoring winger from Dundee United. Then introduced the exciting and immensely talented John Deehan.

As League Cup-holders, Villa competed in the 1975—76 U.E.F.A. Cup. They didn't progress very far, but the experience gained will stand them in good stead for future European campaigns.

Aston Villa, now alive to the ever-changing face of football, are more than equipped to go forward into the 1980s with confidence.

Those ghosts of glories past have been laid to rest at last!

'Villa Park, a stadium fit for a team geared to achieve more success.

Andy Gray, bought from Dundee United.

my side of soccer
GERRY FRANCIS

The life of an international footballer is certainly a roving one ... but very often, on his travels he is not fully aware that he's in a foreign country.

I know from my own experience that all I usually see is the airport, hotel and stadium.

Travelling interests and excites me, and when abroad I try to do as much sightseeing as I can.

The summer of 1973 was the best ever for me. I sampled the delights of Jamaica for the first—but not, I hope, the last—time.

My trip to the West Indies started with the England Under-23's. Our first stop was Ankara, Turkey, which was extremely hot and humid.

We were praying for a drop of rain to cool the air and soften the pitch.

Our wishes were granted a few hours before the match ... but unfortunately the rain just didn't stop.

In the end, it was like a monsoon and the referee was forced to abandon the game at half-time.

He had no option as conditions were farcical.

On the way back from the stadium, we saw that many streets were already flooded with people leaving their cars for the safety of a first—or second—floor home!

"Malcolm Macdonald, Mike Channon and me hold the aces during an airport card game."

'MY SOCCER TRAVELS'

"Portuguese troops provided the background to our match in Lisbon last year."

I've never seen rain like it, and I don't particularly want to again, either.

From Ankara we flew to Belgrade via Athens and Dubrovnik. I liked the Yugoslav capital, which seemed to combine the best of the East and West.

The people were friendly and made us welcome.

We did not play in Red Star's impressive stadium, but a smaller local ground, unfortunately.

Next stop: Valence, near Lyons in France. After our 2-2 draw, I started my trip to Jamaica.

I flew home to Heathrow Airport where I changed on to a Pan-American Jumbo jet bound for Miami.

The flight took over ten hours and not being the best of fliers, I didn't enjoy it. I watched a couple of films, slept when I could but was relieved when we landed in Florida.

I didn't have a visa so I couldn't leave Miami Airport. Instead, I went to the lounge, paid a ridiculous price for a drink and watched T.V.

I saw three hours of non-stop comedy shows . . . I Love Lucy, My Favourite Martian, Laurel & Hardy . . . well, it killed time.

Jamaica is only a short flight from Miami and when I finally arrived in Kingston, I was glad that my journey was over. I felt shattered!

I was, perhaps, lucky that my Queens Park Rangers team-mates had already fulfilled their fixtures, so I spent seven days lazing in Montego Bay—highly recommended!

It was fabulous. If you've ever thought how nice the place looks in the brochures, I can assure you the real thing is even better.

The weather was ideal and I used to eat and sunbathe in the hotel, surrounded by banana trees with a steel band playing and the waves lapping at the beach.

A long way from Shepherds Bush!

Seriously, it was just about the most enjoyable week I've ever spent abroad.

Despite being famed for their love of cricket, the West Indians made us footballers feel at home. There was also no hint of the racial friction that forced us to have an armed guard.

One day, I've promised myself that I'll go back to Montego Bay.

My first-ever trip abroad came with Rangers.

It was a close-season tour of Spain, although I must confess that it is not a place I like.

The food doesn't agree with me and you have to go a fair way south to get away from the hustle and bustle.

I remember playing at a Second Division stadium in Calella, where the toilet facilities were dreadful.

Another early trip was to Gibraltar with an F.A. team. It was just after Gordon Banks had his car accident that ended his career.

Among others in the party were Nobby Stiles and Frank Worthington.

There was a bit of trouble with Spain and the borders were closed with the army on full alert.

The locals of the British colony really enjoyed seeing us, even though we thumped their team 9-2 or some similar score!

Apart from the West Indies, I must list Scandinavia as my second favourite, especially Norway and

"In action against Czechoslovakia in Bratislava, my first match as captain of England in a competitive international."

Sweden.

Rangers are very popular over there and we received good support when we played.

The countries were very clean and just about everyone speaks good English, which is a big advantage.

Other countries I've visited with the club are Holland, Belgium and West Germany, where we slammed four goals past Borussia Mönchengladbach.

My first trip abroad with England was to Switzerland. I was carrying a heavy cold and my schedule was: bed, the game, then back to bed.

Czechoslovakia was rather more hostile, especially as that vital European Championship tie approached.

Bratislava was an unhappy place . . . I could sense an air of depression.

Lisbon gave us a warm-hearted welcome even though Portugal was suffering domestic upheaval at the time.

There were quite a few troops at the ground, but the troubles did not interfere with the football thankfully.

Most of my holidays in recent years have been spent in the South of France, where I own some land.

I usually stay in a small town called Le Lavoudu just outside St. Tropez. As yet, I haven't run into Brigitte Bardot, though . . .

I thoroughly enjoy myself down there; I like the originality of the area and I can get away from it all without the fear of meeting lots of people.

Of all the places I haven't been to, I'd like to visit New Zealand most of all.

I'm not likely to go there with football unless Rangers tour Down Under.

South Africa also falls into this category.

There are some South American countries that intrigue me, but, touch wood, my soccer travels should take me there.

Top of my priority list . . . Argentina during our summer—their winter—of 1978 for the World Cup Finals!

See you there,

Gerry Francis

Everyone knows—or should know—that the biggest ground in Britain is Hampden Park, Glasgow, home of Queen's Park F.C. for more than a hundred years. All the British crowd records have been set up at Hampden for Scottish Cup and international games. Even Wembley cannot compare with the Queen's Park ground for attendance figures, although Wembley Stadium with complete cover for the fans is vastly superior to Hampden. (Sorry, Scots, but it's true, isn't it?) But can you name the biggest ground throughout the 92 clubs in the Football League? Wait for it—the answer is the Valley, the south-east London home of Charlton Athletic.

Built in a natural valley with a towering, terraced slope on one side the ground has accommodation for 66,000 spectators, but it's a good many years since the Valley was even half full. Charlton have now sold part of their extensive ground for building development. More's the pity, but then years ago Arsenal—or Woolwich Arsenal as they were then, found it impossible to make ends meet at their ground just a short bus ride from the present Valley. In 1913 they took over the sports ground of St. John's College, Highbury, in north London and moved lock, stock and barrel to make a new start.

It was a wonder move. Today Arsenal Stadium is one of the finest grounds in the League with accommodation for 60,000 and amenities comparable with a first-class hotel. The Gunners also have the nearby London Transport station named after their ground "Arsenal Stadium". Even Spurs, whose ground at White Hart Lane is almost within shouting

dered why so many clubs' grounds records are far higher than their official capacity figures of modern times. The answer is simple. Over the years clubs have installed new and larger stands with more and more seating which cuts down considerably the number of fans who can be accommodated. Other restrictions have been forced upon the clubs by police and local government authorities for safety reasons, so very few clubs except perhaps among those in the lower sections of the League, can ever hope to break attendance records.

For these reasons there are now only five clubs with a 60,000 ground capacity—Arsenal, Bolton Wanderers, Charlton Athletic, Chelsea and Manchester United. Even Everton, with a record gate of 78,000, and Liverpool (62,000) cannot now accommodate crowds of more than 58,000, although their local derbies could attract nearly twice that number.

What amazing progress has been made on Merseyside over the past century. At first there was only one club on Merseyside, Everton. They played on several grounds before they took over a field in the Anfield Road at a rental of £100 a year! That was in 1884. The team did well, the club prospered and the ground was developed. Then in 1892 their landlord demanded an increased rent. Everton refused and sought another field in the Goodison Park area. It was a desolate waste but with much toil and sweat it soon assumed some semblance of a football ground. Today, with stands on all four sides, it is one of the finest grounds in the League. But so is Anfield. When Everton left for Goodison a

Around the

range of Highbury, cannot make a similar claim, although their headquarters has undergone amazing changes since its inception in 1898. Originally the ground was a market garden growing tomatoes mainly, at the rear of the now famous White Hart Hotel. Today Spurs' ground has a 56,000 capacity although their record crowd is over 75,000, set up in March 1938, which is 2,000 more than Arsenal's best ever attendance in 1935. You may have won-

new club was formed to take over the ground, a club named Liverpool. The fans on Merseyside are proud of their two great clubs for no city in England can boast two finer football grounds.

But what about Manchester, you may ask? All right, no one will argue about that. City's ground at Maine Road, where a record crowd of over 84,500 watched a Cup-tie against Stoke City in March 1934 was taken over by the Blues in 1923. It has one of the largest playing pitches in the League, 117 yards long and 79 yards wide. Only Doncaster Rovers' Belle Vue ground can beat those measurements—118 yards x 79 yards. As a comparison, Derby County's pitch measures 110 yards x 71 yards, and Manchester United's 116 yards x 76 yards.

(Left) One of the finest grounds in the League—Highbury Stadium, home of the great Gunners. Present ground capacity is 60,000, but the record attendance is 73,295 v. Sunderland for a First Division match in March, 1935.

Unlike Arsenal and Spurs, or Everton and Liverpool, whose grounds are within walking distance of one another, Manchester's two grounds, at Maine Road and Old Trafford, are at opposite ends of the city. Old Trafford, home of United, was taken over in 1910 and cost £60,000 to equip (a fortune in those days but not enough to buy one top class player in modern times!). But during the war the ground became a target for Hitler's bombers and when football was resumed in 1945 Manager Matt Busby took over a mass of twisted wreckage and a pitch that resembled a rubbish dump. It was impossible for United to resume football under such terrifying conditions, but their Manchester City neighbours came to their rescue and offered to share Maine Road with the Reds. It was a wonderful gesture so for more than a season, while Old Trafford was rebuilt, Matt Busby's United played ALL their matches "away from home". Today Old Trafford, with its own railway station just outside the ground, houses bigger crowds over the season than any other ground in the country.

Not many clubs have had the same ground throughout the whole of their career but Bury are one of the exceptions. When the club was formed in 1885 they leased a field on one of the Earl of Derby's farms—it was known as "Mr. Barlow's field, Gigg Lane", and although it had a haystack where one corner-flag should have stood and a row of trees along one touchline, they turned it into a football pitch. That same field is now a very fine ground with its own social club and all the usual amenities for public functions.

to ground in south-west London they were offered a home alongside the Thames at Putney. It was part of the spacious grounds of the Craven Cottage estate. The actual "cottage", in which Bulmer Lytton wrote that epic book "The Last Days of Pompeii", remains to this day as part of the football ground, although it is now dwarfed by the stands and terracing.

The fans of old would be staggered if they could see the way so many of those old-time grounds have been developed over the years, particularly in the way of grandstands. For instance, Chelsea's ground at Stamford Bridge, originally built as an athletics arena, now has one of the most up-to-date stands in the country, with sumptuous, centrally heated private boxes for wealthy supporters, who can dine while they watch. Other clubs are installing sports complexes with gymnasium, squash courts, social clubs and high class restaurants, all for the use of supporters and their families. The modern fan demands comfort, unlike their grandfathers who were prepared to stand out in the rain and cold to watch their favourite teams in action. But modernisation costs big money so only the wealthy clubs can afford to develop their grounds in this way.

It is a far cry to the days when the captain of the original Woolwich Arsenal side sat at the entrance to their field to take the "tanners" from the fans before the game began. Or can you imagine modern Arsenal fans paying an extra sixpence to sit on a plank perched on an Army ammunition wagon at the side of an open field—their first grandstand? How times have changed....

grounds

Derby County's first ground was on the local racecourse but in 1895 they took over the ground of a baseball club that had failed to draw the crowds. Hence the name of County's headquarters—the Baseball Ground.

No League club ground had a more romantic start than that of Fulham. After flitting from ground

Wembley—regarded by many as the Mecca of English football. With completely covered accommodation it is superior to its Scottish counterpart, Hampden, (above, right), in most respects. Hampden can hold more fans. Old Trafford (below, right), the most famous club ground in England, has been completely modernised, houses over 60,000 fans, and is a setting worthy of Manchester United's exciting team.

Everything in the garden seems rosy for Wolves striker John Richards and his wife Pam. Despite a disappointing 1975/76, John is still one of the League's top stars. John made his Wolves debut in 1969/70 and in 1972 played on the England Under 23 summer tour. The following season, John was Division One's top scorer. During the Home Championships of 1973, John won his first full England cap against Northern Ireland. John has also helped Wolves to a League Cup Final triumph.

DEREK PARLANE
RANGERS

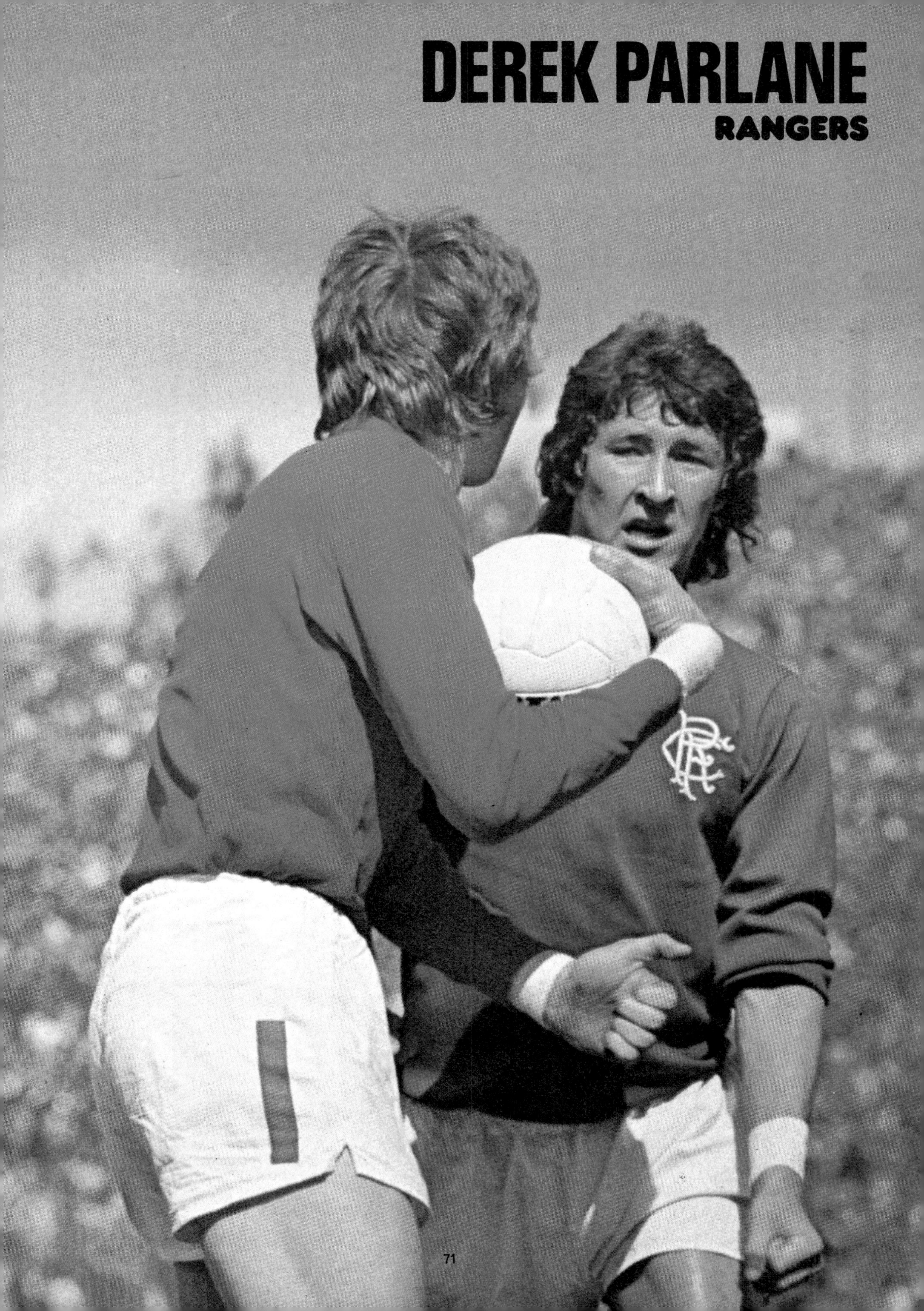

THEN

A young Vic Halom (right). He starred for Charlton, Orient, Fulham and Luton Town before moving on to Sunderland (left) where his goals helped the Roker Park club to achieve F.A. Cup glory in 1973.

Bobby Moore needs no introduction. Above, we see him in his very early days with West Ham. The England record cap holder joined Fulham (right) in March, 1974.

Leeds United's tough-tackling star Norman Hunter (left) joined the club straight from school. He made his League debut in 1962-63 and has never looked back. He has since made well over 500 League appearances for the Elland Road club and has been capped 28 times for England. He's still a happy player (below), despite his reputation as a "hard man".

Charlie George (below) pictured during his early Arsenal days. He helped the Gunners to a League and F.A. Cup "Double" in 1970-71. In the summer of 1975, George (right) was transferred to Derby where he became an instant success.

and NOW

Norwich and Scotland goalscorer Ted MacDougall (above) has seen service with six League clubs. He began with Liverpool but didn't make the first team. Ted then moved on to York, Bournemouth (right), Manchester United and West Ham.

Ipswich and Northern Ireland star Allan Hunter (above) made his international debut v. Russia in 1970. Previously played for Oldham and Blackburn.

Brilliant Trevor Francis (left) hit the football headlines when, as a raw 16-year-old, he scored 15 goals in 21 outings for Birmingham during 1970-71. Francis played a major role the following season in helping his club gain promotion to the First Division. Won his first England under-23 cap v. Denmark in November, 1973. Now he is mature in every respect.

GARY JONES
EVERTON

ALEX RENNIE
DUNDEE UNITED

'Some of my GOLDEN

"Give the ball to the glove" . . . that used to be a memorable shout round Ibrox Stadium not all that long ago. The accent was undoubtedly Fife and the player doing the calling was certainly sure of his ability.

That player was one of the greatest I have ever seen—the amazing, the incredible, the astonishing, the incomparable Jim Baxter, a player of all talents. "The glove"—as he called it—was his left foot. And when it was brought into action it was a breathtaking sight . . . a deadly menace to rival defences.

Baxter was a player the world admired and I have many fond memories of him. Don't get me wrong, though. It wasn't all sheer delight playing beside Jim.

There were times you would look for him in a defensive position— AND THERE WOULD BE NO SIGN OF HIM! Jim would have sauntered off into attack and stayed there when the other team broke from defence.

That was Jim, though. That was what made him extra-special. A character. A personality. The fans will never forget him and neither will anyone who either played with or against him when he was at his peak.

Remember his display against England at Wembley in 1967? Scotland won 3-2 that day—I'm sorry I keep reminding English soccer fans of that score!—and Baxter and Denis Law were both at their brilliant best.

I think Scotland could have beaten any team in the world that day. Yes, even Brazil, West Germany or Holland. We had the incentive and the motivation. England had won the World Cup the previous year and they were still unbeaten—until that day.

We went on to Wembley knowing that even our own fabulous fans would have been quite content with a draw. I'll never forget that Scottish team. It was: Ronnie Simpson; Tommy Gemmell, Eddie McCreadie, myself, Ronnie McKinnon, Jim Baxter, Willie Wallace, Billy Bremner, Jim McCalliog, Denis Law and

outside Ibrox chanting "Jim Baxter . . . Jim Baxter." Taxi drivers were stopping on their way past giving a big wide grin and a thumbs up sign to any Rangers player they saw. You would have been forgiven for thinking Rangers had just broken the world transfer barrier!

But, here was Baxter returning on a free transfer and he was still doing it in style. Only Jim could have created such a stir. I'm sorry things didn't work out for him on his return

John about to tackle Sabo of Moscow Dynamo in the memorable European Cup-Winners' Cup Final in 1972.

Bobby Lennox. What a line-up that was!

Law and Lennox put us 2-0 ahead, then England pulled one back before McCalliog, making his international debut, went through to smash a third goal away from Gordon Banks. England scored again, but there was no way we weren't going to win.

If England had even hit an equaliser in the last two seconds I would have felt quite confident that either Slim Jim or Denis would have scored another in the last second. It was that sort of day.

I know a lot of English players and fans never forgave Baxter for his mickey-taking that day. Shortly after that game, Jim was transferred from Sunderland—the club he joined from Rangers—to Nottingham Forest for over £100,000. Whenever he attempted things and they didn't come off he was hammered. Eventually he was given a free transfer and returned to Ibrox.

I'll never forget that day when Jim came back. There was a huge crowd

to Ibrox. Everyone had hoped he would be a big success, but, alas, it just didn't work out that way. But I'll always remember Jim at his best, weaving magic all over the pitch with "the glove".

Like I said earlier, Jim could get you annoyed with his antics on the pitch. His tackling was never in the Norman Hunter class, but everything he did was part of that aura. He used to have words with players after games, but one thing he never did was hold a grudge. He might have an argument one night, but next morning he would breeze in with a big smile—and the feuding would be over.

Jim Baxter was one of the good things about soccer I remember. There are lots of other things that bring a smile to my face when I recall past events in this wonderful game.

Right up there at the top of the pyramid of pleasure is the European Cup Winners' Cup victory over Moscow Dynamo in Barcelona four seasons ago. That was a night that will live with me forever. It was really quite amazing—a game that seemed to flash past in the opening hour then drag out the remaining 30 minutes.

Colin Stein put us 1-0 ahead with a raging right-foot shot that no goalkeeper on earth could have stopped. Then Willie Johnston made it 2-0 . . . and then Johnston struck again to make it three. We were moving the ball about sweetly, everyone wanted to be involved in this glorious night.

Then Moscow Dynamo pulled one back. The Soviets hit another near the end and we really had to sweat it out before the referee eventually blew the final whistle.

The next thing I remember was being mobbed by fans. Now I know how a pop superstar feels! I could hardly move for well-wishers. A picture appeared in one of the daily newspapers of this huge fan giving me a bear-hug and I had a pained expression on my face. What a way to

argue with the official. The game eventually went to extra-time . . . and it was then that we lost it.

Franz Roth was left with an opportunity and he flicked the ball over the head of goalkeeper Norrie Martin for the only goal of the game. I was sick.

Anyway, I've got plenty of happy memories. I'll never forget my last-minute goal against Italy in the World Cup qualifying game at Hampden in 1965. Just about every Scottish player seemed to be involved in that move as

MEMORIES'

celebrate a European trophy victory!

That was actually our third Cup-Winners' Cup Final. We lost the first —a two-legged affair—to Fiorentina and then we met Bayern Munich in West Germany in 1967 on a dreary night in May. Obviously, we were at a disadvantage right away because the game was virtually a home game for the Germans. The European

Union had decided the venue right at the start of the tournament and they refused to change it even after Bayern won through.

That was one game that will not join my happy memories. We had the ball behind Sepp Maier when big Roger Hynd scored—but the referee decided it was offside. I thought it was touch and go, but you can't

it went down the right flank. Billy Bremner, Neil Martin and Jim Baxter all seemed to have a touch before it was sent across and there was yours truly—at right-back that night!—appearing in the centre-forward position to hit the ball first-time past the goalkeeper.

And on the same ground I'll always remember Kai Johansen's winning goal against Celtic in the Scottish Cup Final replay in 1966. The first game had been drawn 0-0 and Celtic were favourites to win the second game. And then came Johansen's marvellous goal. It was swept across from the left wing, half-cleared by the Celtic defence and there was Kai coming storming in to slam the ball past a helpless Ronnie Simpson from about 20 yards.

I think I could fill this entire book with all my memories, but I had better stop now before Kevin Keegan, Kenny Dalglish and Gerry Francis complain about me hogging all the space!

One of the greatest players John has ever played with—Jim Baxter—scores from a penalty given against England in 1963. It won the game for Scotland.

TONY TOWERS
SUNDERLAND

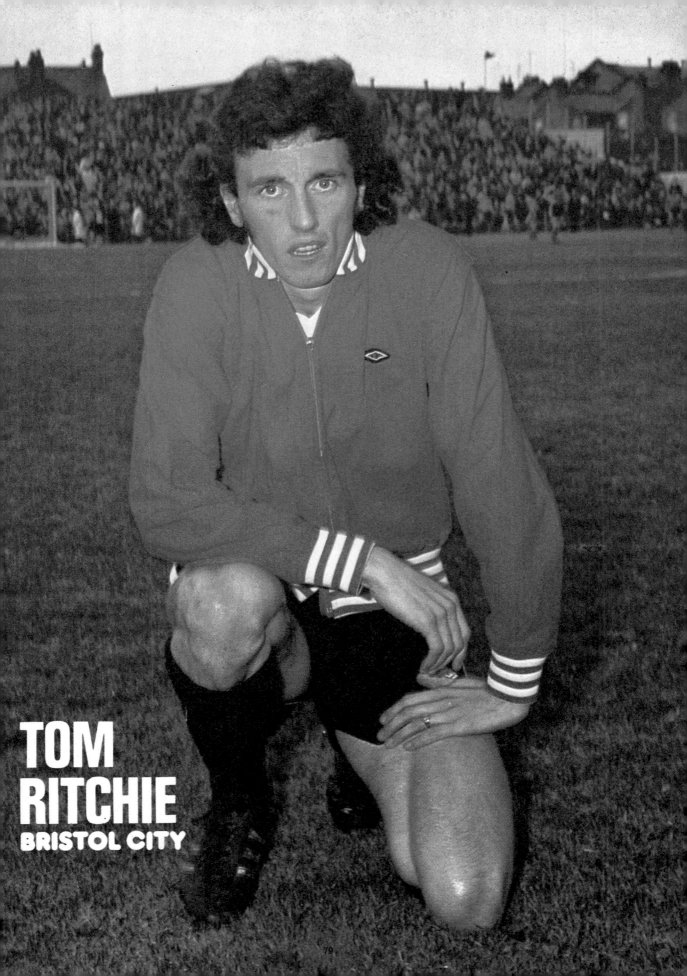

TOM RITCHIE
BRISTOL CITY

Tommy shows 'em how!

Giacinto Sarti had never witnessed a shot of such awesome power. The pulverising pace of the mighty right foot swing sent the ball hammering high into the net . . . a devastating, unstoppable drive.

The man who scored that memorable goal was Tommy Gemmell, Scottish soccer's laughing cavalier of a player. That goal came against Inter-Milan in the European Cup Final in Lisbon on

May 25, 1967, and brought the score back to 1-1 before Stevie Chalmers hit the winner near the end.

Gemmell was a Celtic player then—a spectacular, raiding left-back whose fierce drives struck terror into even the bravest of goalkeepers. A lot has happened to Gemmell since he left Inter's superb goalkeeper Sarti helpless that day.

He has the distinction of being the only British player to score in TWO European Cup Finals—he hit another long range drive against Feyenoord a couple of years later, but Celtic lost 2-1

after extra-time—and he has also been on target in the Intercontinental Cup Final when he scored with a penalty-kick against Racing Club in South America. Unfortunately, Celtic didn't win that trophy either as the third and final game developed into a farce with FOUR Parkhead men being sent off and Racing winning 1-0.

"I'll never forget that game," recalls Gemmell. "To refresh your memory Celtic won the first leg at Hampden 1-0 with a goal from Billy McNeill. In the second leg in Buenos Aires we were leading 1-0 after I had scored with a penalty-kick.

"Then the South Americans scored from a position that was at least six or seven yards offside. We couldn't believe it when the referee allowed it to stand. Remember, we had lost our goalkeeper Ronnie Simpson before the match when he was hit on the back of the head by a metal object thrown from the crowd. Reserve John Fallon had taken his place.

"The South Americans tried every dirty trick in the book to unsettle us, but we kept our tempers. Then they scored another goal and the game had to go to a play-off in Uruguay.

"That game has since been called the 'Second Battle of the River Plate.' It was never a football match. We just weren't allowed to play and, unfortunately, four of our players—Jimmy

Johnstone, Bobby Lennox, John Hughes and Bertie Auld—were ordered off.

"Racing Club scored the only goal of the game, but it was during yet another break in play that my infamous moment arrived. They had a player called Raffo —a cunning, vicious man.

"I saw my chance during the break. I ran at him and gave him a swift boot in the behind. Before the referee could turn around, I had retreated to a safe place. Okay, I realise what I did was utterly wrong and had nothing whatsoever to do with football— but then a lot Racing Club did had nothing to do with the game.

"I thought I had got away with it . . . unfortunately I had forgotten all about the television cameras. Boy, did I feel silly when I was told about it."

Gemmell—one of the greatest characters in world soccer—has also sampled English football with Nottingham Forest before returning to Scotland with Dundee.

The Dens Park fans took to him immediately and within a year Gemmell had skippered the team to a 1-0 League Cup Final victory at Hampden—beating, of all sides, CELTIC!

"I've a few good seasons left in me yet," says crackshot Tommy. "I'm still as enthusiastic as ever. When I look around and see all the good young players coming through I realise I have a job to do. Someone's got to show them how to play, haven't they?"

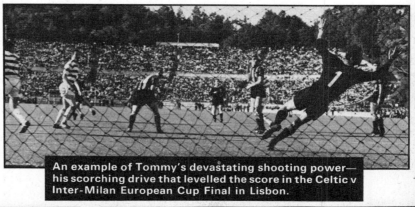

An example of Tommy's devastating shooting power— his scorching drive that levelled the score in the Celtic v Inter-Milan European Cup Final in Lisbon.

Burns beats injury jinx

From Manchester United to Preston North End via Southampton. That briefly is the story to date of Francis Burns, a fullback-cum-midfielder whose form as a regular with the Old Trafford brigade was good enough to earn him a full Scottish cap.

Still only in his mid-twenties, the quietly-spoken Scot points to a run of bad luck and injuries which have dogged him along the way . . . reasons, he feels, why he never became a household name with Britain's number one club.

"I'd reach a stage where my game was good and I was an established first-teamer. Then injury would force me out," recalls Francis.

"I've had all four cartilages removed, three of them before I was 21.

"I could have played for United in their greatest triumph to date, the winning of the European Cup in 1968 against Benfica.

"I was a regular up until after the first leg, Semi-Final match against Real Madrid. Then the jinx struck.

"The previous year the club went on a close-season tour of Australia. I was just beginning to enjoy myself when a leg played up."

In August, 1972, battler Burns left the famous Red Devils to sign for Southampton. And again fate dealt a cruel blow.

"After only six weeks in the South I went down with another bout of cartilage trouble. Following my recovery I tore my right thigh muscle.

"My problems didn't end there. The family and I just couldn't settle in Southampton. It came as a relief when I was given an opportunity to head back North and sign for Preston.

"That was in August, 1973. Bobby Charlton had become the new manager, his first such post, and two other old team-mates of mine, David Sadler and Nobby Stiles, were on the books.

"It was a challenge I relished, one good reason being I couldn't possibly suffer from cartilage trouble again. They'd all been taken out!"

The slightly-built Scot then went on to compare Sir Matt Busby and Bobby Charlton, no longer at Preston, as managers.

"Matt was always the same and will never change. I can give you a perfect example.

"Last season a testimonial match was staged at Old Trafford for Paddy Crerand. The European Cup winning squad of 1967/68 played the then-present first-teamers.

"Matt was in charge of us old uns and gave a typical team-talk. 'Let the ball do the work,' he said. It was just like the old days.

"Bobby didn't set out to be a carbon copy of Matt. Whilst allowing some of the great man's methods to rub off on him, he introduced ideas of his own. He set out to be a manager in his own right, not wanting to be compared to anyone else.

"It was a pity a question of principle forced him to resign from Preston."

Had Francis any regrets about leaving Manchester United?

"At the time of my departure I was a little bitter. Frank O'Farrell had the 'hot-seat' in those days and felt there was no future for me at Old Trafford.

"Things have since worked out well, although it's taken some time. I'm enjoying my football more than I ever did.

"I'm an older, wiser player and the youngsters at Deepdale seek me out for advice. They know I've been at the top, even if I didn't stay there.

The never-say-die spirit of Francis Burns will help Preston to become proud again.

local boy makes good

David Harvey–Leeds–

The understudy who learned from the stars' mistakes

Though David Harvey is a Scottish international goalkeeper, he was born in Leeds (February 7, 1948) and has supported the Elland Road lads for as long as he can remember.

Now he's a superstar, with memories galore—including getting rave write-ups for his part in Leeds' 1972 Cup Final win over Arsenal.

He's a quiet man who lives with his wife and two children on a small-holding in East Yorkshire, surrounded by animals—calves, pigs, hens, and retired greyhounds. To relax from the split-second decisions he makes in game after game for Leeds, he likes to go hunting for rabbits or hares.

For that, he needs patience. And David Harvey has always had to show patience, specially in his job as a professional footballer.

David joined Leeds as a 15-year-old, after being spotted in schools' soccer with Foxwood Secondary School in Leeds. He signed on, full of confidence about making the grade—but six years later, when he was 21, he was still in reserve football with the club.

Reason was the sometimes brilliant, occasionally shaky, form of Welsh international 'keeper Gary Sprake. David watched Sprake make superhuman saves, then let in an easy shot—just through a lapse in concentration.

And local boy Harvey taught himself to concentrate harder than anybody else through those long seasons in the Central League.

When Sprake was eventually transferred to Birmingham for £90,000, the Welshman had played nearly 400 League games for Leeds. And David Harvey had had but 30.

He'd stepped in for the injured Sprake in the 1970 Cup Final replay against Chelsea, which the Londoners won. Then came the triumphant display against Arsenal two seasons later—and a first cap for Scotland in a World Cup qualifying tie against Denmark, November, 1972.

Scotland qualified, of course. And the ever-patient Harvey was voted best goalkeeper of the 1974 World Cup Finals in West Germany.

Harvey's own biggest hero is Johnny Giles, for so long the master-mind of Leeds' mid-field. Giles was a perfectionist, so is Harvey. He says: "Every time I let a goal in, I give myself a right old telling off. I tell me just what I should have done to stop it. And then I'll go away and practise doing it the right way."

At the club, they call David Harvey "suave" . . . because he admits he's somewhat scruffy.

Really he is a back-to-nature sort of character. He'll trudge round the countryside in his "wellies" but he says: "It all helps me as a footballer. If I can relax the way I like, then I'm that much fresher when the time for the next game comes around."

Having to wait so long for a chance to play for his beloved Leeds has made David Harvey very grateful for the good things football has given him. "But when I get home, it's like moving into another world, a complete contrast."

David so far has two daughters. Maybe one day he'll have the son he very much wants. "If he wants to follow in my footsteps, that's fine. If football doesn't appeal, then that's fine too. But if he does turn professional, I hope it'll be with Leeds.

local boy makes good

Phil Thompson–Liverpool–
From fan to F.A. Cup Finalist

Phil walked up the steps to the Royal Box at Wembley to collect an FA Cup winner's medal for the part he played in Liverpool's sensational win, 3-0, over Newcastle United.

He walked up, feeling no tiredness in those spindly legs which had caused Liverpool boss Bill Shankly to say: "He must have tossed up for those legs with a sparrow—and lost."

Thompson had played right through Liverpool's Cup campaign, and missed only seven games in the League campaign which had seen the Anfield heroes end in second place, behind Leeds.

But the Final was the big dream. Says the thin but tenacious Phil: "Liverpool have been my team for as long as I can remember. I was born in Kensington, part of Liverpool, in January, 1954. By the time I was five I had a dream, which was always with me . . . even when I was supposed to be doing my school-work.

"I wanted to wear a Liverpool shirt. And I wanted to win something with the club. Just signing for the club as a kid was enough excitement for me to think my heart was bursting with pride. And I've never regretted a single moment of my life—even when I was in the F.A. Youth Cup Final in 1972, but finished on the losing side.

"If you have the determination and the talent, then Anfield is a footballer's dream world. The training staff there have always been great for me, and that great old Liverpool hero Ian St. John was specially kind and helpful. Nothing is too good for a Liverpool player, and it makes you determined to play your heart out for the club in every game."

Phil's debut for the Liverpool League side was part-way through the 1972-73 season when Shankly pushed the lanky lad—he's a six-footer but weighs only a shade over 10 stone—into an important away game against Norwich. Liverpool got a point in front of a full-house crowd to hang on to their position at the top of the table.

He was to get eleven other outings in that season which Liverpool ended as Champions, holding off the Arsenal challenge. The previous season he'd made one appearance on the substitute's bench—to the confusion of quite a few fans.

Confusion? Well, that fine winger Peter Thompson was still with Liverpool in those days—so to mark the difference, Phil had to be named in the programme as P. B. Thompson.

Now Thompson says: "If football is in your blood, then I suppose you'd play anywhere for anyone. But to find a place in the team you've idolised for years and years really is very special.

"The Anfield crowd really urge you to give your best all the time. They're fair, too—opposing sides get credit when they do well.

"I don't suppose I'll ever experience anything like what happened after we'd won the Cup that day. On the train, I could feel the tension building once we'd left London. By the time we'd got to Crewe, there were supporters galore just come to

meet us half-way.

"And the city itself was just a sea of red and white."

Now Phil Thompson hopes for more honours for the team he supported as a kid. The feeling of being a local boy who really makes good hasn't worn off yet, but he's also got his eye on a full cap for England.

"Though I don't suppose it'd be any more exciting than pulling on that red shirt of Liverpool for the first time," he says.

Brian Talbot–Ipswich–
Still in love with Portman Road

Ipswich-born and proud of it (birth-date July 21, 1953), Brian remembers with special pleasure the very day he made his first-team debut for Ipswich Town. It was against Burnley, at Turf Moor, and Ipswich nicked the points.

Eighty first-team games later, Brian played for his long-time favourite club in a League Cup match away to Leeds—and broke his left leg.

It was a sad hold-up in the career of a young player who had so early been tipped as a future international. But the Talbot determination to get back in an Ipswich shirt helped recovery . . .

Brian Talbot, local boy who made very good, could hardly have been more "local"—he was born five minutes' walk from the Portman Road ground. He says: "I really love the place. You hear doubts about whether top players would want to be out in the sticks here in Ipswich, but I can assure them it's a fantastic place to be."

When Sir Alf Ramsey was managing and masterminding Ipswich to a first-ever League Championship in the 1961-62 season, having pushed them to promotion only the season before, Brian Talbot was only eight years old.

"But I knew then, as I got involved in any kind of soccer kick-around I could find, that what I wanted more than anything else was to play for The Blues. My dad really encouraged me to make the grade."

So it was that Brian would often play two games on a Saturday, and still fit in a visit to see Ipswich play, and then another one on the Sunday. In fact, Ipswich took Brian straight from school. There was a time, a dreadful time, when he was put on the transfer list.

Nobody went in for him. But Brian arranged, with manager Bobby Robson, to have a couple of summers playing for Toronto in the North American League. "I might have been a bit of a country boy up to then," he says, "but the travelling and the new scenery and the experience really did make me a much better player."

Of his own game he says: "I'm not one of the highly-skilled fancy players. I'm a trier. I'll give as much effort as anybody."

That Brian is a confident player is seen by the way he shows no nerves when he takes penalties for the club. As for his general performances, manager Bobby Robson says of the local lad: "He hasn't exactly got a heart—it's more a couple of engines placed inside his shirt."

Nothing upsets Brian—except a situation where Ipswich could have won something but, for whatever reason, didn't. Like the club's fine F.A. Cup run the season before last when, after three replays against Leeds they got to the Semi-Final, only to lose to West Ham in another replay, this time at Stamford Bridge.

And they just faltered in the League title run-in finishing third on 51 points along with Liverpool, just behind Derby County. And worst of all the previous season when Ipswich lost in the Quarter-Finals of the U.E.F.A. Cup to Lokomotive Leipzig . . . on penalties!

Says Brian: "I can take personal bad luck. But if Ipswich get any, then it really hurts me. But then I was the same way when I was a starry-eyed kid out there on the terraces."

Keith Osgood—Spurs—still feels the urge to yell

Mike England was on his way away from the club.

Osgood, nearly six-feet tall and a muscular 11 stone 2lb, found himself playing not just for his own place but for the very future of the club. Spurs eventually escaped relegation, but only by one point over Luton Town and Chelsea.

doesn't score, of course, and barely gets a look in. But I nip upfield for the winner . . . the one that gives us the Cup."

And he adds: "Spurs have been an important part of my life for years and years. Even in League games, I find myself sometimes yelling 'Come on The Lilywhites'."

'Come on the Lilywhites'

Southampton's Peter Osgood has scored well over a hundred League goals in his spectacular career which started with Chelsea. But at the time when the yells of "Osgood IS good," or "He's the wizard of Os" echoed round First Division grounds, there was another Osgood waiting in the wings.

Keith Osgood, now happily settled in as a Tottenham Hotspur regular. Another local boy who learned to love football early in life—and went on to play for the team he's always supported.

They're not related—except in the sense that Keith Osgood also was originally in the goal-scoring business. He says: "In the days when I was just a Spurs fan and an amateur player, I banged in quite a few goals up-front with London Boys, then Middlesex Boys and finally England Boys. I got a few more up-front for the England Youth team.

"It's a good feeling, banging in goals. It's true that the goal-getters are the glamour boys, and that the game is all about goals. But there's a lot to be said for stopping them, too, and I'm completely happy about the fact that I'm now a defender in the First Division."

The flavour of top-level life with his much-loved Spurs came as substitute in the very last game of the 1973-74 season. He didn't get on in that 2-0 away win against Newcastle. And Spurs finished the campaign in a comfortable mid-table berth.

He started the next season with a couple of games, but had to wait seven months before getting back the number five shirt when

Says Keith: "It would have broken my heart if we had gone down, specially having just started to establish myself in the side. But it must be obvious that Spurs just have to be a First Division side—the whole club, the whole atmosphere at White Hart Lane, smacks of top football."

From the middle of the defence, Keith Osgood has changed role somewhat to come more into a semi-sweeper position, with the increased opportunities for going forward and recapturing some of that old goal-scoring knack.

Like most young players, Keith names one established star who had a particularly strong influence on him. "It has to be big Mike England. He was world-class.

"I'd watch every move Mike made—how he'd get into position, how he'd time his tackle, how he'd get up to head the ball. He got a few goals during his time with Spurs, and I hope I can do as well as he did."

Keith is a Londoner who went to school in Isleworth, Middlesex. That he's got fighting spirit was proved by the way he held his own against the challenge of the Scottish international Willie Young, bought by Spurs to strengthen the defence for a matter of £100,000.

Says Keith: "I've often had this dream of Spurs meeting South-ampton, or wherever Peter Osgood may be at the time, and having the job of marking him. He

1. *It`s not a satellite*

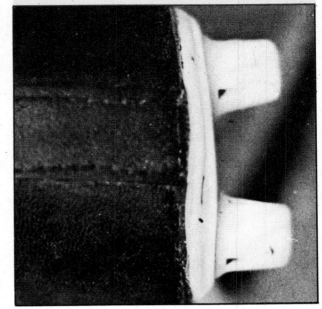

2. *What a fast striker shows a slow defender*

Study the photos and the cryptic clues to name these familiar objects found at big matches.

PUZZLE

Solutions on page 125

5. *Sharpshooters` target*

6. *Grandstand view from here*

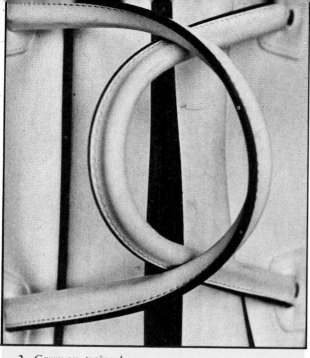

3. *Carry on, trainer!*

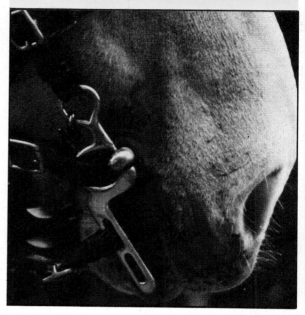

PICTURES

7. *Worn—and waved!*

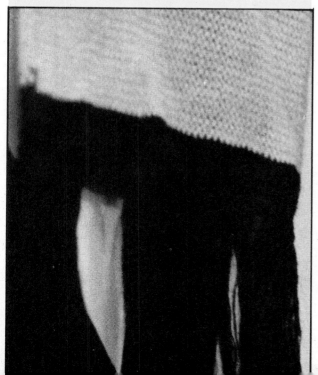

8. *Keeps fans in their places*

YOU ARE THE REF

1 A penalty-kick has been awarded. The original 'keeper, who had been replaced after an injury, asks if he can go back into goal for the penalty. What is your answer?

2 The ball is shot towards goal and is clearly about to enter the net. Before it passes over the line a spectator runs on to the pitch and deflects the ball away from the goal. Do you award a goal or not?

3 In a junior match a player, unable to play because he's under suspension, is produced to act as a linesman. Anything wrong?

4 You observe a player receiving treatment on the touch-line. He has one foot on the pitch. Is this allowed?

5 At the kick-off, the ball is touched by a second player before it has rolled completely off the centre-spot. You stop the game and award . . . ?

6 A goalkeeper intentionally throws the ball hard into the face of an opponent. What action do you take?

7 You have blown your whistle for a penalty-kick to be taken. You then see that the goalkeeper is not standing on his goal-line. Do you stop the kick and order him on to his line?

8 A defender, taking a direct free-kick outside his own penalty-area, passes the ball back to his goalkeeper who misses it and the ball rolls into goal. What decision do you make?

9 A goalkeeper dives for the ball as it is about to leave his penalty-area. He grabs it when it is half-way over the line. What is your decision—penalty, free-kick outside the area, or do you wave play on?

ANSWERS

1 · 2 · 3 · 4. yes, you do not award a goal. Law 14, requires you to restart by dropping the ball at the spot where the spectator interfered with play. **3.** Players may not act as a linesman or a referee during suspension. **4.** No. The player must leave the pitch (with your permission) to be treated and must await your signal before rejoining the game. **5.** You do not award anything, but order the kick to be taken correctly.

clearly that you must not stop the kick, but Law 14, International Board Decision No 2, states No. If outside the area—a direct free-kick. **7.** No. in the penalty-area you would award a penalty-goalkeeper must be sent off. If the offence occurred into the opponents' half. **6.** This is equivalent to striking an opponent and is violent conduct. The distance of its circumference i.e. about 27 inches the ball is not in play until it has travelled the

await the outcome. If it does not result in a goal the kick must be retaken. **8.** Correct decision is a corner-kick. From a direct free-kick a goal can only be scored against the offending side. **9.** Play on. The ball must be completely over the line before is considered to have left the area.

Morton's promising youngster Ross Irvine

ON THE SPOT

A famous nursery for promising youngsters — that's Morton. The Cappielow club—expertly run behind the scenes by supremo Hal Stewart —have never been afraid to give youth a chance.

Two Anglo strikers who first came to the fore at Morton are Leeds' Scottish international leader Joe Jordan—who cost the Elland Road club only £20,000 when he was transferred five years ago—and Donnie Gillies, who cost £35,000 and scored that sensational winning goal in the English F.A. Cup for Bristol City against mighty Leeds four seasons ago.

JOE JORDAN OF LEEDS CAME TO THE FORE AT MORTON

STAN RANKIN

Now there are more youngsters on the glory trail at Cappielow. Starlets determined to break the barrier into the soccer big-time. One such player is Ross Irvine, a versatile and clever player who can operate with expert ease in midfield and the back-four. Here, in an exclusive feature he has a discussion with Stan Rankin who has been with the club for over 10 years since signing from juvenile side Glasgow United.

IRVINE: What sort of advice would you give to a young player coming into the game today, Stan?

RANKIN: Firstly, the boy must be dedicated to the sport. He may have been the best player in the school team or a juvenile side, but when you join a League outfit you must be prepared to start again. You must prove you are good enough to be in this company.

IRVINE: And what about fitness?

RANKIN: This is undoubtedly another important aspect to a youngster's play. You can have

puts his veteran team-mate Stan Rankin

all the skills and a good football brain, but you must be able to last the entire 90 minutes. A youngster may find it a bit of a strain at first. After all, he's competing against players who have trained daily throughout their careers. These players should be in peak condition—a young lad will have to work hard to get in that shape.

IRVINE: You helped me a lot when I first came into the team, Stan, and I'll always be grateful. What do you think a young and inexperienced player should do at the start of a game when nerves are most likely to affect him?

RANKIN: That's easy, Ross. I

ROSS IRVINE

would tell him to do the simple things. Make sure he hits the target with his first touch of the ball. Make it a simple pass to a colleague. Don't be in too much of a hurry to impress—the fans and the team-mates realise the situation and they will be patient.

IRVINE: What is the worst thing a young player can do?

RANKIN: The exact opposite of what I have just said! If a teenager comes into the team, tries something clever in front of goal, is robbed and the other team break away and score, his game is likely to go to pieces.

IRVINE: Which youngsters have impressed you during your stay with Morton?

RANKIN: Ross Irvine—a great player! Seriously, though, I think wee Neil McNab had a great debut for the club and he didn't look back after that. He gained in strength right from that first game.

IRVINE: Is there anything in particular you remember about his debut?

RANKIN: It was against Partick Thistle at Firhill and it looked as though it would be a tough one for us. Neil looked so frail and thin-looking as he stripped for the game that we all wondered how he would make out. Obviously the boy had talent, but he had still to prove it.

IRVINE: And how did he prove it?

RANKIN: He went on to that park and demolished the Thistle defence! I think we won by four goals that day and Neil—at only 15—was rated our top man. He was always in space looking for the ball and when he got it he wasn't afraid to go at players and

put pressure on opponents. It was no surprise when he signed for Spurs the following season. I think Neil has a big future.

IRVINE: Any last word of advice for a budding soccer genius?

RANKIN: Yes, never stop listening to advice. I've been in this game for long enough now, and I'm still learning. Once you think you know it all you are in trouble. Even the great Pele once said there is always something fresh and exciting to be learned.

IRVINE: I won't argue with that, Stan. Anyway, thank you very much for the hints. I hope other young players—like myself—take heed of your words of wisdom.

NEIL McNAB IS A CAPPIELOW PARK PRODUCT

England's captains since the War

Billy BEATS Bobby

Gerry Francis is the 16th player to have the honour of leading England since peace-time international matches restarted in 1946 after the Second World War.

The Q.P.R. skipper, however, has a long way to go to beat the record for captaining England, held by two men.

First Billy Wright led the way when he skippered England 90 times and Bobby Moore ended his England leadership on the same total.

GEORGE HARDWICK was the first England captain. George won 13 full England caps and all as skipper. A tall, handsome footballer who spent most of his career with Middlesbrough.

It is unusual even in League football for a goalkeeper to be captain of his club. But FRANK SWIFT, so tragically killed in the Munich air crash in 1958, had the honour of captaining England twice in 1948-49 and needless to say "Big Swifty" celebrated by keeping a clean sheet in both games. Frank won 19 full England caps.

Then, spanning a period of 11 years, BILLY WRIGHT led his country. Billy was the first player to win 100 caps for England—he ended with 105, and an England team without his name between 1947-59 was a rare sight indeed.

Billy had an amazing run of 70 successive matches as skipper, a record that will surely stand for all time.

Billy Wright was once in charge for 70 consecutive games.

First at wing-half and then at centre-half, Wright was always the heart of England's defence.

ALF RAMSEY also captained England. Later he was to earn fame as manager of England's World Cup winning side of 1966, and a knighthood.

Ramsey played his international soccer while Wright was skipper, but he did lead England out on three occasions in his 32 appearances.

A cool penalty-taker for club

Holder of a record 108 caps—Bobby Moore.

footballer.

JIMMY ARMFIELD is now at the helm of Leeds United, displaying the same coolness as he did as a full-back with Blackpool and England. Jimmy was capped 43 times and skipper on 15 occasions. Jim was never flustered, no matter how fierce the pressure, and England won ten of the games when he was in charge.

BOBBY MOORE equalled Billy Wright's appearances total, but Billy had that run of 70 consecutive games in charge. Bobby's best run was 27 games.

Bobby, who saw England team-mate Bobby Charlton overtake Wright's total of 105 England games and reach 106, himself overtook Charlton and finished his international career on 108 caps.

The outstanding moment for Bobby, of course, was leading England to the 1966 World Cup triumph.

Whenever England were in trouble, they called up RON FLOWERS. Ron played his first English game in 1955 v France and last ten years later v Norway, yet Ron received only 49 caps. We say only, because in an equal period, other players won far more.

Yet Ron never let England down, and he skippered England three times.

BOBBY CHARLTON was the 10th player to captain England since the Second World War, and did the job three times.

One of the finest ambassadors England have ever had, his play thrilled millions, and many a heart missed a beat as he unleashed those thunderbolt shots that were his trademark.

His 49 goals are a record for England, a total in no danger of being overtaken, either in the near distance or far distance.

ALAN MULLERY, who was to make a fairy-book return to Wembley with Bobby Moore with Second Division Fulham in the 1975 F.A. Cup Final, won 35 England caps.

With Bobby Moore and Bobby Charlton absent, Alan skippered England on one occasion when England beat Malta 1–0 in Valletta. A tireless worker who served England well.

Four times MARTIN PETERS skippered England. Scorer of a goal in England's 1966 World Cup Final victory over West Germany. Martin won 67 caps between 1966 and 1974.

Known as "The Ghost" for his ability to meet far post centres,

and country, Alf netted three international goals.

RONNIE CLAYTON. Between 1956 and 1960, Ronnie played 35 times for England. A consistent and constructive wing-half, he skippered England five times during 1959-60.

Just how many caps JOHNNY HAYNES would have won can never be answered. He had 56 caps and been skipper in 22 games when he damaged his leg in a car crash in Blackpool. An outstanding inside-forward, his long passes to the wing will always be remembered. Another of Johnny's claims to fame is that he was the first £100-per-week

England won 10 of their 15 games under Jimmy Armfield.

Gerry Francis captained his country for the first time in a friendly against Switzerland in 1975.

Martin scored 21 goals for England. In four of those games he was skipper. Martin's record was three draws—v Wales (0–0), Poland (1–1) and Portugal (0–0).

But the other result was a stunning 7–0 win over Austria at Wembley.

A player with tremendous stamina, COLIN BELL was still adding to his impressive total of caps in the 1974-75 season.

Colin skippered England when they lost 1–0 to Northern Ireland in the 1971-72 season at Wembley, a shock result that makes football the great game it is.

EMLYN HUGHES, full-back in that so-successful Liverpool side over the last decade, won 40 England caps between 1970 and 1975, the last being in a 0–0 draw with N. Ireland in May, 1975.

When Joe Mercer was appointed England acting-manager after Sir Alf Ramsey was dismissed, he appointed Emlyn skipper of the England side and he had a run of nine consecutive games in the role.

Hughes had skippered England in Don Revie's first two matches as England team-manager, but it was ALAN BALL who took over for the friendly with West Germany at Wembley and looked set for a long reign as he finished the 1974-75 season by leading England to a 5–1 victory over Scotland at Wembley.

NOT SELECTED

The last survivor of the 1966 World Cup side, Alan had reached 72 caps with that victory. A fine leader and a non-stop worker on the field, his career looked as if it had fallen apart in the summer of 1975.

He asked for a transfer from Arsenal, and having lost his place in his club side for the start of the 1975-76 season, Revie could not select him for England.

Happily for Arsenal, Alan changed his mind about a transfer and by Christmas 1975 was back as skipper of the Highbury club. But in his absence Revie had named GERRY FRANCIS as England captain and given him a year to prove himself in the position.

As England strive for the 1978 World Cup, let's hope Gerry has a photo of Bobby Moore holding the 1966 World Cup close at hand for inspection.

The full record of England's captains

GEORGE HARDWICK
(Middlesbrough)
1946-48 P13 W10 D2 L1 F49 A12

FRANK SWIFT
(Manchester City)
1948-49 P2 W1 D1 L0 F4 A0

BILLY WRIGHT
(Wolves)
1948-59 P90 W49 D21 L20 F234 A135

ALF RAMSEY
(Tottenham)
1950-51 P3 W2 D1 L0 F11 A6

RONNIE CLAYTON
(Blackburn)
1959-60 P5 W1 D3 L1 F9 A9

JOHNNY HAYNES
(Fulham)
1960-62 P22 W12 D4 L6 F64 A31

JIMMY ARMFIELD
(Blackpool)
1961-66 P15 W10 D2 L3 F45 A18

BOBBY MOORE
(West Ham)
1963-73 P90 W57 D20 L13 F171 A75

RON FLOWERS
(Wolves)
1964-65 P3 W2 D1 L0 F4 A2

BOBBY CHARLTON
(Manchester United)
1968-69 P3 W1 D2 L0 F4 A2

ALAN MULLERY
(Tottenham)
1970-71 P1 W1 D0 L0 F1 A0

MARTIN PETERS
(Tottenham)
1971-74 P4 W1 D3 L0 F8 A1

COLIN BELL
(Manchester City)
1971-72 P1 W0 D0 L1 F0 A1

EMLYN HUGHES
(Liverpool)
1974-75 P9 W4 D4 L1 F12 A7

ALAN BALL
(Arsenal)
1974-75 P6 W4 D2 L0 F35 A3

'Keeper the fans bought

Organised walks, wine and cheese parties, and raffles are three reasons why 'keeper Peter Grotier has become Lincoln City's last line of defence.

"It is the most novel form of flattery I've experienced," recalls the Sincil Bank star.

"At the start of the 1974/75 season West Ham loaned me to Lincoln. I was to have been there for a month only but the club were anxious to sign me.

"The only problem was lack of sufficient money to secure my services.

"An advertisement appeared in a local evening paper stating that cash had to be raised if I was to stay at Lincoln. It was an appeal which brought an incredible response.

"It seemed the whole of Lincoln wanted me and every one was determined a deal would be done with West Ham.

"Before I knew what was happening, all sorts of schemes were put into operation, all with the same aim . . . to get the required amount needed to sign me.

"The fans worked like fury. The social side of life in Lincoln boomed and as a result £7,000 was collected. The club put all they could into the kitty—around £13,000—and West Ham's asking fee of approximately £20,000 was met."

Peter then pointed out that he hadn't planned to sign for City, but since doing so has had no regrets.

"I'd got into a rut at Upton Park. Apart from a regular first-team run—I think it was 34 games—during the 1969/70 season I was continually in and out of the senior side.

"There was the added obstacle of having to compete with Bobby Ferguson. Hammers seemed to be going through a permanently poor patch, too. I became disillusioned.

"A loan to Cardiff City came up but it didn't enhance my career. I returned to West Ham and firmly

back to square one.

"I was on the transfer list when Lincoln came along with their proposition.

"Then came what I can only describe as the greatest vote of confidence a player could receive.

"The wife and I love the city and its people. Our respective families live down London way, which means we can't meet as much as we would like to. But when we do visit them—about once a month—our trips to 'The Smoke' are eagerly awaited."

The Imps—as Lincoln are fondly referred to—have never looked back since goal-stopper Grotier came to stay.

Peter is the first to toast the loyal Lincoln folk who wined, dined and walked in order to get their man.

"I only hope I don't play badly enough to force them to raise money for a replacement," chuckled Peter.

Martin has no regrets...

Norwich manager John Bond

When Martin Peters joined Norwich City in 1974/75 after almost 500 League appearances for West Ham and Spurs, many fans thought the one-time England star was on his way down the soccer ladder.

How wrong they were. Martin's arrival, shortly after The Canaries' League Cup Final defeat by Aston Villa, saw their promotion bid move into top gear.

Of course, City eventually regained their First Division place and Martin was back among the "giants". Only his strip had changed!

He remembers: "I was 31 when I moved. The way some critics talked, you'd have thought I was 40!

"I left Spurs because I thought I had gone as far as I could with them. The move suited us both.

"When I joined Norwich, I thought that it was just a temporary loss of First Division status and I was right.

"I knew the manager, John Bond, from my West Ham days. Even then, I admired his approach to the game.

"I was happy to become a Norwich player under John. As an attacker, his go-for-goals tactics suit me.

"If I had any doubts, it was whether my family would settle in East Anglia. After all, we were used to London life.

"To be honest, we're glad to be out of the rat race. The people here seem less rushed and we all thoroughly enjoy living in the Norwich area."

So—no regrets from the player who won 67 England caps in an international career where, looking back, perhaps he was never given the credit he deserved.

"It was a blow when I realised that my England days were numbered," Martin admits.

"I suppose it was inevitable after we failed to qualify for the 1974 World Cup Finals that some players would be dropped.

"I won just three more caps after we drew 1-1 with Poland at Wembley.

"Playing for England is something no player can ever forget. I treasure my World Cup winners' medal.

"Only 11 English players have these. Who knows when more will find their way to England again?"

A fair question. Another question: what will Martin do when he finally hangs up his boots?

"I haven't decided yet. While I love football, I don't know if I will definitely stay in the game as a coach or manager.

"At the moment, I'm enjoying playing so much that retirement seems a long way off."

Martin Peters

Sign of success . . . Billy with an expensive foreign car.

As a wee lad, running about the back streets of Raploch, a tough district in my home town of Stirling, I never dreamt that one day I would be a famous footballer.

You had to be hard in Raploch, so I knew how to handle myself. If you couldn't you never stood a chance when the older and bigger boys picked on you.

Probably because of this background, I lay awake some nights dreaming of becoming a professional boxer and going on to win a World title fight.

Next to football, boxing is my

"LIFE AT THE TOP HAS BEEN GREAT"

great love. Mention Muhammad Ali and I'll talk all day and night.

As it's turned out, though, success with Leeds United and an international career with Scotland has brought me fame and fortune.

It's been a great life. I own a lovely house on the outskirts of Leeds, drive an expensive car, wear the latest clothes, travel everywhere first-class, eat in the best restaurants and have provided a good standard of living for my family.

My wife Vicky doesn't have to watch every penny when she's out shopping. My kids have the best money can provide.

Not that we are spendthrifts and the children are spoilt. It's simply that we are able to ensure they are well-clothed and fed.

Thanks to a bumper testimonial in 1974, my family's future is secure. If any of my kids want to go on to a higher education I'll be able to provide for their studies and see they get a good start in life.

Perhaps I've been lucky along the way, but I haven't got all these benefits without a lot of hard work over the past 16 years or so.

Although I've benefitted from the game, I like to think I've given Leeds United, Scotland and the fans full value for money.

Nobody gets something for nothing in this life, especially footballers.

The playboy stars are soon found

Billy in World Cup action v. Yugoslavia in 1974.

No star treatment for players such as Crewe's Hugh Reed.

out. Sure, they might earn big money for a while, but very few manage to stay at the top for more than a couple of years.

I also never lose sight of the fact that only a tiny handful can earn a great deal from this game.

The majority of players in the Third and Fourth Divisions would be better off with a job outside.

There are those in the lower Leagues who have to take on other work to supplement their wages.

Several I've heard of, for example, are window cleaners, painters, decorators and minicab drivers.

It makes me annoyed when people class all footballers in the big money League.

Take it from me, life can be very hard for a player with the Darlingtons, Scunthorpes and Crewes of this world.

Not for them the bright lights, expensive cars, houses in the stockbroker belt. They struggle to make a living out of the game they love.

Even so, I believe many professional footballers at the top are underpaid.

We are entertainers, playing to packed houses every Saturday. Fans come from miles to see us in action.

Our earnings are generally unrelated to our crowd-pulling power.

If, say, Leeds were playing at home to Liverpool in a vital Championship match, the gate would be around 45-50,000.

Probably the TV cameras would also be there, to boost the audience to around ten million.

When I read about the huge contracts showbusiness stars can command for just one performance, and then take a look at what the majority of footballers are paid, the comparison makes me annoyed.

Like showbusiness personalities, many of today's leading footballers can earn additional money. Sponsoring sportswear, opening boutiques, pubs, garages and appearing in adverts on TV.

Quite a few top-liners have business interests, usually in the sports and fashion worlds.

Some, like Colin Bell, own restaurants. Others such as Geoff Hurst, Peter Storey, Jim Baxter and Frank McLintock have invested some of their money in public houses.

I have no other interest off the field—apart from a newspaper column and writing for SHOOT/GOAL weekly. All my energy has been concentrated on playing football.

In the past my agent has often telephoned me asking if I'd endorse some product or other.

I've refused every time because I didn't want anything to distract my attention from Leeds United.

Former England star Geoff Hurst pulls pints in one of his pubs—the Sheet Anchor in Staffs.

'LIFE AT THE TOP HAS BEEN GREAT' CONTINUED

I did agree to do one TV advert, though for the gravy people.

It involved my wife and kids and I simply fancied seeing how a TV commercial was put together.

Most top stars earn a lot of extra cash opening supermarkets, fashion shops, garages and pubs. I haven't done anything like this, for the past three or four years.

It's not that I don't enjoy meeting people, it's simply that I prefer not to be in the limelight.

In my opinion this is one of the disadvantages of being a leading figure in sport.

To me the whole business is embarrassing . . . you just don't have a private life.

I place tremendous value on my family and usually keep them and my home separate from football. You won't see any photos of my lounge or kitchen in some women's magazine.

I can't take Vicky out for a quiet meal without being pestered all night for my autograph, or some complete stranger treating me like his long-lost brother and trying to tell me what's wrong with the game.

We can't even make a quick shopping trip without being continually jostled and stared at.

Many top stars, like Malcolm Macdonald, own boutiques.

I know many are true fans and are well-meaning, but I bet they wouldn't like their privacy invaded every second of the day.

Most fans believe a top footballer's life is all glamour. They think we are members of some great international jet-set.

The only jets I see are the ones which have taken me and my team-

An incident from the 1975 European Cup Final, when Leeds lost 2-0 to Bayern Munich. Most players just dream about soccer at this level:

mates to other countries to play a match.

Sure, if you are with a top club and play at international level you do travel a great deal, but you rarely get the chance to see much of other countries. You normally arrive the day before a match and leave directly after it. Often there's not enough time to dash off to the local shops to buy presents for your wife and kids, let alone go sightseeing.

Anyhow, I'm not a good traveller and can't wait to get home after a trip abroad.

Apart from the financial rewards, success at home and in Europe are meat and drink to a top professional. The thrill of winning the League title or F.A. Cup, the tremendous feeling

of achievement reaching a European Cup Final, is beyond price.

When I think the majority of players will never play in the First Division or at Wembley I sit down and give thanks that I've spent my career with a club as great as Leeds United.

As I said earlier, my life at the top with Leeds and Scotland has been very rewarding, and I'll always be grateful to everyone: players, managers, directors and fans who have helped me along the way.

All the best . . .

Billy Bremner

A reward for life at the top . . .
F.A. Cup triumph in 1972.

Some players are destined to spend all—or most—of their years in League football with one club. But there are others, men with well-known names, too, who never stayed long with any club yet earned a reputation for their dedicated enthusiasm and a do-or-die professional attitude to their game no matter what coloured shirt they were wearing. We might call them "Soccer's S.O.S. men" for they were always ready to answer the call of any club manager who had need of such a dependable character to help him in a promotion or relegation battle.

These "happy wanderers" are playing—and have played—a very important role in their own particular way. There is no better example than wee Willie Carlin, that tough, tenacious little midfield workhorse who had eight different clubs during a remarkable career. Born on Merseyside he won an England schoolboy cap in 1956 and was signed by Liverpool, but he left Anfield in 1961 without having tasted League football and joined Halifax Town. Still the sun didn't shine on wee Willie. Then in 1964 he moved on to Carlisle United to help the Cumbrians in their quest for promotion from Division 3. At the end of that season

HAVE BOOTS, WILL TRAVEL

Soccer's happy work-horse wanderers

United were Champions and no one had done more to make this possible than the little Merseysider.

Next he answered Sheffield United's S.O.S. but was unable to prevent The Blades dropping from Division 1. But Brian Clough, then manager of Derby County, secured the little man for £63,000. It was a wonder move for club and player. Willie

(Left) Willie Carlin has won honours with many clubs. (Right) All-action Trevor Hockey appeared in over 500 League games for seven clubs.

Carlin's terrific work-rate as a midfield power-house helped Derby to the Second Division Championship. Two seasons later Leicester City took the step-up to the top class—and the man of experience and inspiration who led the climb to the top was wee Willie. Yet his wanderings weren't over. He moved again to Notts County and in the 1972-73 season gained his fourth promotion medal, for County rose from Division 3. Little Willie Carlin ended his incredible career with Cardiff City who signed him in the hope that his magical charms would work for them in

102

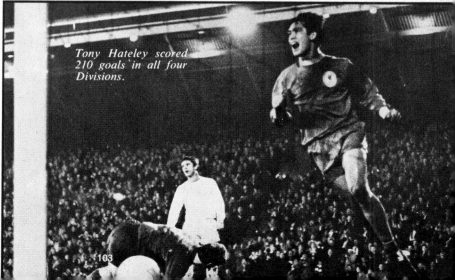

Bobby Kellard has fought in many relegation battles for different clubs.

their struggle for Division 2 survival. Unfortunately the battle was lost and the Welshmen were relegated. The happy wanderer had reached the end of the long road.

Trevor Hockey is a member of the "have boots, will travel" brigade. Up to the end of the 1974-75 season the fearsome, bearded man-of-all-work had appeared in well over 500 League games with seven clubs covering something like 16 seasons. He began with Bradford City, had a spell with Nottingham Forest and then with Newcastle United whom he helped to win the Championship of Division 2 in 1965. Next came Birmingham City where he was appointed captain and then he answered the call of Sheffield United who wanted him to mastermind their bid for Second Division promotion.

It worked a treat. United returned to the upper class with Trevor Hockey. Norwich City were next to send out an S.O.S. for the tough wandering warrior in their struggle to retain their place in the top class after being promoted the previous season. Trevor did it. Relegation was warded off but within a few months, after he had gained his first international honours—with Wales, he was off again, this time to Aston Villa. Unfortunately, he was unable to work the

miracle at Villa Park and before the Claret and Blues finally made it back into the upper class, Trevor Hockey had returned to his first love, Bradford City. He never really became famous but his name will never be forgotten as one of Soccer's happy wanderers.

Men of steel and stability, capable of instilling their own indomitable fighting spirit into their team-mates may not reach international status but their worth to their clubs is invaluable. Take Bobby Kellard, that tough little fellow with the heart of a lion. He played with six different League clubs starting with Southend United at the age of 17. Then followed a "Cook's Tour" around the country and most of his moves were to clubs who had urgent need of his dogged determination. From his home town Southend he went to Crystal Palace and in 1964 helped the Londoners into Division 2.

But his stay was short and on he went to Ipswich, then Portsmouth and to Bristol City, to skipper the side. Leicester came next and promotion to Division 1, but it wasn't long before Crystal Palace, in relegation danger persuaded him to return to Selhurst, take over as skipper and save their position in the First Division. He did it, too, but during the following season he answered the relegation S.O.S. of another of his former clubs, Portsmouth—and again worked a miracle.

In more recent times we can instance the experience of Dave Lennard who had worn the colours of Bolton Wanderers, Halifax, Blackpool and Cambridge United before he was recruited by Chester in Septem-

ber 1974. With his experienced, inspiring determination he revitalised the side and not only did Chester reach the League Cup Semi-finals after shock wins over Leeds United and Newcastle, but earned them promotion to Division 3 for the first time in the club's history.

When Birmingham City signed Bob Hatton in 1971 he was joining his fifth club in seven seasons. The others were Wolves, Bolton, Northampton and Carlisle. With those clubs Bob was always a good player but not outstanding, but his move to Birmingham transformed him into a very fine goalscoring striker and at the end of that first season City were promoted to Division 1.

For many years now the crying need of most managers has been to find goalscorers. Tony Hateley was top of the "wanted" list during the '60's and he became a happy wanderer solely because of his goal flair. In all he scored 210 goals in League football with clubs in all four Divisions— Notts County, Aston Villa, Chelsea, Liverpool ,Coventry City, Birmingham City, back to Notts County and finally Oldham.

The same was true of Hugh McIlmoyle. The Scot wandered far and wide in search of goals— Leicester, Rotherham, Carlisle, Wolves, Bristol City, Carlisle again, Middlesbrough, Preston, Morton and Carlisle for a third time. When Carlisle were in need of a striker they sent for Hugh McIlmoyle—but when they signed him for the third time his magic didn't work. They were relegated from the top section. Even the happiest wanderer must eventually end his travels and sit back with his memories.

Tony Hateley scored 210 goals in all four Divisions.

NEVER MIND THE WEATHER...
The game goes on

Tom Finney, the famous Preston and England winger, makes a splash against Chelsea.

Birmingham City's Trevor Francis pauses for thought during a rain-swept game.

Soccer water-polo! Nat Lofthouse, the great Bolton striker, is tackled by Chelsea's Peter Sillett in a 1957 League clash.

Workmen clear rain from the pitch at Frankfurt before the start of the 1974 West Germany v. Poland World Cup tie.

S(no)w business like snow business . . . but Arsenal's under-soil heating ensures the snow doesn't turn to ice and the match against Southampton carries on.

Leeds 'keeper David Harvey shows a safe pair of hands as he grips the greasy ball.

Alone in the rain— Bryan Hamilton (now Everton) in action for Ipswich in a U.E.F.A. Cup tie in Rotterdam against Feyenoord.

To most of us the Soccer term "hat trick" means three goals by one player in the same match. It once meant three in a row but now the "hat-trick medal" is awarded to every player hitting three goals in a game. If that is true then we can attach the term to all sorts of other occasions in football, but first let us look at a few real "three-on-the-run" hat tricks.

Huddersfield Town hold the distinction of being the first club to achieve the Championship hat-trick when they won the League title in 1924, '25 and '26. Since then only one club has equalled that remarkable performance—Arsenal, who held the top team trophy in 1933, '34 and '35. Alex James, tiny Scots midfield wizard, was the idol of the Highbury fans during that incredible three-season run of success when the Gunners scored a total of 308 goals.

Wolves might have emulated the Huddersfield and Arsenal three-in-a-row Championship feat when they took the title in 1958 and 1959, led, of course, by Billy Wright, and were favourites to win it again the following year. But like the two-goal striker who misses his hat-trick by hitting the woodwork in the last few minutes, Wolves had the title snatched from them by Burnley by just a solitary point. So bang went a Molineux hat-trick of Championships.

Leeds United can claim a First Division hat-trick although Don Revie, Billy Bremner, Jack Charlton, Allan Clarke and Co. did not derive much pleasure from it. United were Championship runners-up in 1970, '71 and '72.

Old Firm 'Double'

Plymouth Argyle can look back on an even more incredible performance. In the days when there were two sections of Division 3 (North and South, with only the top team of each section winning promotion, Argyle achieved a double hat-trick by finishing as runners-up SIX seasons on the trot (1922 to 1927).

Up in Scotland Rangers and Celtic have achieved all sorts of hat-tricks both in the League and the Scottish Cup but then they have dominated the game North of the Border for so long that this is not really so remarkable. Yet we should mention the fact that Rangers have performed a Cup hat-trick three times (1934-36; 1948-50 and 1962-64). Both Rangers and Celtic have done what no English club has achieved and that is to win all three of their National trophies—Championship, F.A. Cup and League Cup—in the same season. In fact, each have done it twice.

When it comes to the F.A. Cup only one Football League club has ever achieved a hat trick of Final

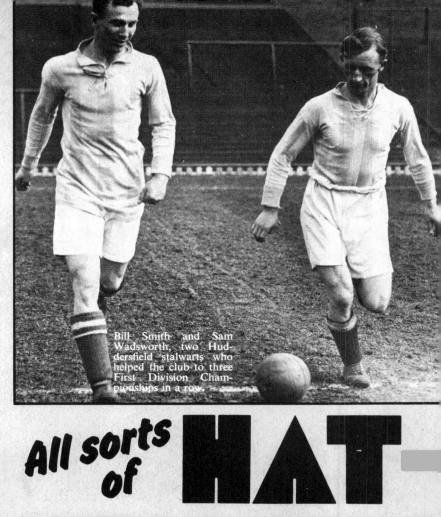

Bill Smith and Sam Wadsworth, two Huddersfield stalwarts who helped the club to three First Division Championships in a row.

All sorts of HAT

triumphs but that was 90 years ago when Blackburn Rovers won the trophy in 1884, '85 and '86 at Kennington Oval, home of the Surrey County Cricket Club. Since then no team has ever taken the trophy three times in a row, but Bolton Wanderers deserve a hat-trick medal for being the first club to win three Wembley Finals—1923, '26 and '29. Five players appeared in all three Finals to accomplish a gold medal hat-trick—Dick Pym, the fisherman goalie from Exeter; Jimmy Seddon; Harry Nuttall; Norman Howarth and Tommy Butler.

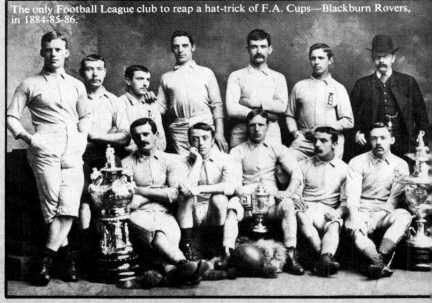

The only Football League club to reap a hat-trick of F.A. Cups—Blackburn Rovers, in 1884-85-86.

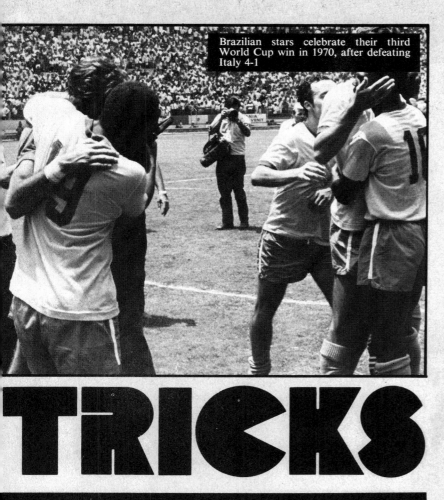

Brazilian stars celebrate their third World Cup win in 1970, after defeating Italy 4-1

TRICKS

achieved another "all together" hat-trick when they appeared in Leeds' three U.E.F.A. Cup (Fairs Cup) Finals—in 1967 when United lost to Dynamo Zagreb, and in the two winning Finals of 1968 (v. Ferencvaros) and 1971 (v. Juventus). That was also another hat-trick record, for Leeds are the only English club to appear three times in any of the European competition Finals.

But when it comes to Europe, what about that amazing threesome Real Madrid achieved when they won the European Cup in each of the first three seasons of its existence, and went on to make it five wins in a row? Then there was the Ajax hat-trick of three European Cup triumphs in successive seasons—1971, '72 and '73 in which the Dutch ace Johan Cruyff played such an important part.

Wembley Three

But perhaps the greatest of all was Brazil's three World Cup victories. In the third of these truly superb triumphs, 1970 in Mexico, Pele and Co. took the Jules Rimet Trophy back to Brazil where it will remain for all time.

Let us return to Britain for a few more examples. Sheffield Wednesday hold a record that is somewhat unusual. On three occasions they have been relegated from First to Second Divisions, only to regain their place in the top class within one season. They won't mind remembering that at Hillsborough in spite of their drop into the Third Division. But some of the "relegation hat-tricks" are not likely to bring happy memories. For instance, there was the occasion in 1921 when Bradford (now no longer a League club) dropped from the First to the Second Division. The following season they slipped again, down to the Third. That same season their neighbours Bradford City were relegated from the First Division. A remarkable hat-trick for the football fans of Bradford.

Even that wasn't so bad as the experience of Crewe Alexandra, who finished bottom of Division 3 (North) three seasons in succession—1956, '57 and '58. A few years previously Walsall had suffered a similar hat-trick of misery. They ended 1952, '53 and '54 at the foot of Division 3 South and, like Crewe later on, had to seek re-election.

We'll end on a few goalscoring hat-tricks. Who was the first man to hit three in a match in a Wembley international? Alec Jackson, flying Huddersfield Town winger, for Scotland against England in March 1928. The first Englishman to do it was Roy Bentley, of Chelsea, against Wales in November 1954. The first player to score three in a Wembley Cup Final was Blackpool's Stan Mortensen against Bolton Wanderers in the Stanley Matthews' Final of 1953.

Leicester City also achieved a "first ever hat-trick" but it's not one they would want to remember. They were the first club to leave Wembley three times as losers in their first three Finals—1949, '61 and '63.

Here's another rather interesting hat-trick. Can you name the three half-backs who appeared in three Wembley Cup Finals for the same club? The answer is Billy Bremner, Jack Charlton and Norman Hunter, who formed Leeds United's middle-line in the beaten 1965 and 1970 sides and in the winning team of 1972. But wait, that's not all. That trio

In the 1953 F.A. Cup Final at Wembley, Stan Mortensen's hat-trick of goals helped Blackpool beat Bolton 4-3. Here Stan goes flat-out scoring the equaliser.

EUROPEAN HOT-SHOTS

Ruben Ayala

JOHAN CRUYFF
Holland

Surely the most talented forward to emerge in recent years? Cruyff showed in the 1974 World Cup Finals that he can do things most players only dream of. He has announced that he will not play in the 1978 World Cup Finals, which will be a big handicap for the Dutch.

With Ajax, he won three European Cup-winners' medals, help-

Johan Cruyff

At first, he caught the eye because of his long, flowing hair, which hung below his shoulders.

Now, Ayala has cut his hair (it's still longer than most players', though) and is noticeable for his lightning wing-dashes.

Ayala joined Atletico from San Lorenzo in his native Argentina, and it was unfortunate that he was sent-off in that ill-mannered European Cup-tie against Celtic in 1974. Unfortunate, because most of his team-mates were far worse behaved.

Ayala was outstanding for his country during the 1974 World Cup Finals, but as Argentina have announced that they will call on only home-based players for 1978, his international future may be limited.

OLEG BLOCHIN
Dynamo Kiev & Russia

One of the few—and arguably the best—of the left-footed strikers on the scene. Russian football dipped after they reached the 1972 European Championship Final, but they are back to their best now with the fair-haired Blochin the star attraction.

Blochin made his name in the 1972 Olympics team and was voted European Footballer of the Year in 1975.

He has helped Dynamo Kiev to Championship victories, topping the Russian goal-charts.

Heads . . . it's Oleg Blochin

ing them to become the last truly outstanding European club side.

A near £1 million fee took him to Barcelona and in his first season, the Spanish outfit won the title.

Cruyff is also a very intelligent person and is virtually fluent in English, German and Spanish.

DRAGAN DZAJIC
Bastia & Yugoslavia

Dzajic was just 17 when he made his debut for Red Star of Belgrade. Since then, he has helped them to many honours and has won more caps for Yugoslavia than any other player.

In 1973, he broke a leg, but recovered to lead Yugoslavia in the World Cup Finals the following year.

A left-winger of speed and grace, Dzajic is now 30, but hopes to be around for the next World Cup Finals.

Dragan Dzajic

RALF EDSTROM
PSV & Sweden

Nicknamed the "Man With The Golden Head", Edström is undoubtedly one of Europe's top strikers. He created a big impression with Sweden in the '74 World Cup, while his form for Dutch club PSV has been of a consistently high standard.

Born in October, 1952, Edström made his name in Sweden with Degerfors and Atvidaberg before going to Holland in the summer of 1973.

A central striker, Edström is a gifted all-round player with superb heading skills and a stinging shot in either foot.

ROBERT GADOCHA
Nantes & Poland

Robert Gadocha

Now 30, Gadocha is one of the finest players to emerge from Poland over the years. A natural left-winger, he may not score too many goals, but few flank-men create as many deadly openings as Gadocha.

He won an Olympic gold medal in 1972 and as Poland became a force in world soccer, Gadocha attracted offers from western clubs.

He had a superb World Cup in West Germany. Later, he joined

Master in the air . . . Ralf Edström

107

EUROPEAN HOT-SHOTS
CONTINUED

Another goal for Dudu Georgescu (number eight)

Nantes in France . . . after helping his previous club, Legia Warsaw, knock them out of the U.E.F.A. Cup !

RUUD GEELS
Ajax & Holland

Now accepted as one of Europe's top marksmen, Geels was born in Haarlem and joined Feyenoord at an early age.

Unfortunately, Ove Kindvall was Feyenoord's centre-forward in those days so Geels did not get a chance to establish himself.

Geels left the Rotterdammers for Go Ahead (now called Go Ahead Eagles). He did well and in fact scored twice in a game against Ajax . . . Ajax's only defeat of that season—1971/72.

The blond striker then moved on to Belgian club FC Bruges. Again, Geels found himself pushed into the background by established stars, so in 1974 he returned to his native Holland and Ajax.

In his first season, he netted 34 goals in all competitions out of Ajax's overall total of 91 . . . a very good average.

Last season, Geels led the way again but his moment of glory came when he scored an incredible five goals in Ajax's 6-0

defeat of old rivals Feyenoord.

Geels became a regular choice for Holland and although not a brilliant player technically, he is very consistent and has that golden knack of being in the right spot at the right time.

DUDU GEORGESCU
Dinamo Bucharest & Rumania

Dudu was Europe's top scorer in 1974/75 with 33 League goals, which won him the Adidas Golden Boot award.

Strictly speaking, the Rumanian is not a striker . . . he operates in midfield, but as his goal-tally suggests, frequently joins his front-runners.

He began his career with Progresul and in 1973, went on loan to FCM Resita, who were struggling to avoid relegation.

Dudu scored seven goals in 12 games, which went a long way towards Resita's survival.

In the summer of 1973, he

joined Dinamo and has since become one of the most consistent scorers in Europe.

JUPP HEYNCKES
Borussia Mönchengladbach & West Germany

Jupp has been second only to Gerd Müller in the West German goal-stakes in recent years.

While Gerd is the top Bundesliga scorer of all-time with around 300 goals, Jupp is in second place, about 100 behind but comfortably ahead of other challengers.

The 31-year-old Borussia striker has helped the West Germans to become a force in European football, a fine achievement considering Mönchengladbach is a relatively small town.

Heynckes has never really had the success at international level that he has with Borussia, but is not far short of his 50th cap.

Ruud Geels

Jupp Heynckes poses the keeper a few problems.

Although Heynckes missed out on Germany's 1974 World Cup triumph, he has played his part in their European Championship success.

GRZEGORZ LATO
Stal Mielec & Poland

Top scorer in the 1974 World Cup Finals, Lato is possibly the fastest winger in Europe . . . indeed the world. Anyone who saw him causing havoc in West Germany would agree.

Aged 26, Lato will never be forgotten by England fans. It was his burst down the wing at Wembley in 1973 that allowed Domarski to score Poland's "killer" goal in the 1-1 draw.

Lato's goals have helped Stal establish themselves as one of Poland's top teams.

GERD MÜLLER
Bayern Munich & West Germany

After 62 games and an amazing 68 goals for West Germany, "Der Bomber" decided to retire from international football.

Müller certainly went out at the top . . . his last contribution was to score Germany's winning goal in typical style during the 1974 World Cup Final.

Since Müller won his first cap in 1966, he has gone on to become the most consistent scorer in European football.

His international record will probably never be equalled and he has scored more Bundesliga goals than any other player in the West German Super League.

Club honours include Championships, Cup wins and, of course, European Cup triumphs.

Gerd Müller celebrates a goal.

ANDRZEJ SZARMACH
Gornik & Poland

Szarmach was virtually unknown before the 1974 Cup Finals but, filling in for the injured Lubanski, made an immediate impact and finished high among the goalscorers.

In fact, he was the successor to the great Lubanski at club level, too.

Dangerous in the air, Szarmach is also very difficult to mark.

Poland strikers Grzegorz Lato (left) and Andrzej Szarmach prove a handful for the Italy defence.

Go For The Double

After solving the clues in this specially compiled crossword, you can use the letters in the thick-edged squares to form the name of a Queens Park Rangers and England star (*Answers on page 125*)

ACROSS

(1) Alan —, Manchester City midfield player.
(5) — Rioch, Derby County midfield star.
(9) — Glover of Leicester City
(10) —yn–c–stle Park, home of Hearts
(11) Duncan F––bes of Norwich City.
(12) Look after — as the groundsman does the pitch
(13) Kevin —, Derby County striker.
(14) Personal pronoun from C––ster.
(15) Tip found in the headline "England cap Exeter player"!
(17) "To leave" from Bobby ––uld of Wolves.
(21) How the losing team's fans might feel.
(22) Enjoyment or amusement.
(23) Opposite to 14 from Allan –unt–– of Ipswich
(24) Coven––– City.
(25) Don Mass–– of Q.P.R.
(26) Tony Po––ll of Norwich.
(27) Take four letters (in the correct order) from Ken Burns (Birmingham) for cakes.
(29) Ted Hem––e– of Sheffield United.
(31) Leeds United full-back (4 & 6)
(33) Bill –gham of Burnley.
(34) Joe –o–l– of Manchester City
(35) Martin —, Norwich City midfield star.
(36) Digits of the feet.

DOWN

(2) Steve D–––y of Wolves.
(3) Alan —, Newcastle United full-back.
(4) Preston North —
(5) Mike Summer––– of Burnley.
(6) Run very fast — in competition, perhaps.
(7) Mick —, Coventry City full-back.
(8) T–––y Yorath of Leeds.
(10) Arsenal nickname. (3 & 7)
(12) Might be proposed and drunk to the winning team.
(16) Derek —, Scottish international and Rangers star.
(18) Chris J––es of Spurs.
(19) Not those missing around from S––n–ou––muir of Scotland!
(20) Surname of Eddie or Frank of Leeds.
(22) The number of clubs relegated from the Third Division at the end of a season.
(27) "Sky" colour of Coventry City.
(28) Colche–ter United play at L––er Road.
(30) Mixed-up and missing obsolete musical instrument from C––sta– Palac–.
(31) Leighton –h–lli–s of Aston Villa.
(32) The goal one was patented by Mr. Brodie of Liverpool in 1890.

Phil refused to go to Scotland!

Phil Parkes was on holiday when he first heard that Queens Park Rangers were interested in him.

A Walsall official phoned Phil with the news.

"Sorry, I don't want to go to Scotland!" was his reply.

If Phil's soccer-geography was poor, there is very little wrong with his goalkeeping. Since signing for Rangers in May, 1970 for £15,000, he has become one of the country's top 'keepers.

His captain Gerry Francis says that Phil can become the best in the world.

And last season, Don Revie wrote in an article: "I have seen Phil on a number of occasions lately and it is difficult to find any faults."

Praise indeed and, not sur-prisingly, Phil is flattered by all the compliments.

"I work hard in training and put a lot into my game," he says. "When people like Don Revie say nice things about you, it makes all the effort seem worth-while.

"The most important factor, though, is that if I am playing well, the team must benefit.

"I must confess that I have been pleased with my form over the past year or so.

"During the summer of 1975, I had an operation to remove a small piece of bone from my left knee.

"I had been playing in some pain. I knew I wasn't really 100 per cent fit. This affected my confidence.

"It was a simple operation and a complete success. I started 1975/76 in a much better frame of mind and when Don Revie gave me the nod to recall me to the England scene, it was just fabulous."

Phil realises that the competi-tion for England's goalkeeping jersey is pretty hot.

"I love playing for England. When I won my first cap against Portugal in 1974, it was a personal highlight.

"I try not to think about international football, however. It is easy to become disappointed and Rangers occupy most of my thoughts.

"I remember watching the 1974 World Cup Finals on tele-vision. It must be every player's ambition to take part in the competition.

"I would dearly love to be there with England in 1978, although that's a long way off."

Phil's rise to the top is the result of dedication and, as he said, hard work.

When reporters give Phil the "Man of the Match" award, he will still spend the next week brushing up on some weakness from the match that everyone else missed.

"I'm very self-critical," he con-fesses. "I want to improve all the time."

It comes as no surprise that Phil, who has one of the surest pairs of hands in the business, is also a good carpenter.

The Parkes home in Bucking-hamshire boasts many self-made fitted wardrobes and other things.

Phil ought to think about making himself a cabinet for his England caps and other honours.

Quite a sizeable one, we'd suggest . . .

Phil prepares to avoid the challenge of Birmingham's Peter Withe and kick the ball upfield to start a Rangers' attack.

It's Man. United's Scottish international
Lou Macari on the ball against Wolves.

MIKE CHANNON
SOUTHAMPTON & ENGLAND

"He's a most thorough trainer—makes them rehearse every possible move"

"My skipping rope has got entangled in my hair again, boss"

"Anyone who dodges training does five hours on our moving strip"

"A little idea of mine—a steel cable skipping rope with a 5lb weight welded to it"

117

King of Coventry

For many years, Bryan King was recognised as one of the best goalkeepers outside the First Division. His performances for Millwall had scouts from the top clubs watching him.

Bryan's ambition to play in a higher grade of football came true just before the start of the 1975/76 season when Coventry signed him.

He took over from long-serving Bill Glazier and, as Bryan said after his transfer: "There's only one place to

BOBBY
WATSON
MOTHERWELL

NEAR MISSES

The difference between a goal and no-goal can be so slender. Above, a close-in diving header from Man. City's Dennis Tueart fortuitously falls into the lap of desperately floundering Q.P.R. 'keeper Phil Parkes.
(Below)—Arsenal's Alan Ball is convinced the ball is heading into the net when Burnley 'keeper Gerry Peyton flings out a hand and pushes it over the bar.

You can almost hear the gasps of relief from Rangers' defender Sandy Jardine and 'keeper Stewart Kennedy as this shot from Motherwell's Viv Davidson almost scrapes the outside of the post. Another goal that got away.

(Above)—A full-blooded Trevor Whymark drive from six yards out has Ipswich fans about to shout 'Goal!' But 'Boro 'keeper Jim Platt makes his save of the season. (Left)—One of the reasons why Liverpool lost at Anfield to Norwich last season—Colin Sullivan clears a shot by Ray Kennedy off the line.

Everton 'keeper Dai Davies almost throws his arms up in surrender as barnstorming Billy Bonds unleashes a deadly shot. But one of Dai's arms makes a deflection and denies the West Ham man his goal.

DAVE
CLUNIE
HEARTS

GEOFF NULTY
NEWCASTLE UNITED

'Keeping stars fit needs more than a magic sponge'

by RICHARD ROBERTS, MCSP, Queens Park Rangers' physiotherapist

They used to call us the bucket and sponge men. We were the fellows who ran on when a player went down injured. A quick massage, a drop of icy water down the neck, or in the boot, and all was well again. Or so the popular theory goes.

It isn't true. Oh yes, I know all about the psychological effect of that wet sponge on a bitterly cold afternoon, and sometimes it certainly does work. But there's more, much more, to it than that.

You can be brave as a player and be out of the game for a month or more. You can go out there with a pain-killing injection and, in the long run, do yourself or your team no good at all.

You can train when you shouldn't be training, play when you shouldn't be playing. And, whisper it quietly, you *can* get the wrong treatment.

That's where we come in. No, I'm no witch-doctor, and I don't carry a wand. And I'm not kidding myself that I'm the best in the business. But the letters I'm proud to carry after my name mean that I'm a member of the Chartered Society of Physiotherapy.

It took me three years of hard graft at a teaching hospital to earn those letters. And I mean earn them.

And why not? Today we are dealing with players worth hundreds of thousands of pounds. If they are to earn their salt with the clubs that paid that kind of money for them, they are also entitled to the best possible treatment when they are injured.

I'm no better or worse than the physio' who looks after you in hospital after an operation for a broken leg. I simply chose to specialise in sport because I love it, and football in particular.

I'd like to see the day when every fellow in my job was medically qualified. It's a bit of a pipe dream, I know, because some clubs, particularly in the Third and Fourth Divisions, would find it hard to pay for a qualified man. But it's worth it in the long run.

You see, the important thing about our job is to diagnose the injury. You don't give a player a Codine tablet for a cartilage injury, or strap up his thigh when all he's suffering from is a hangover. OK, that's a gross exaggeration, but you see what I mean.

We have to decide in seconds what damage he has done. And on our decision, plus treatment to come, depends whether that player—and he could be a £200,000 star—is out for two days or two months.

I hope that those of us who work for League clubs who aren't medically qualified, have taken, or intend to take, a course with the F.A. on treatment of injuries. Because it's as much what not to do as what to do.

A couple of summers ago, I was faced with a big problem in Jamaica during Queens Park Rangers' summer tour. Frank McLintock went down and was obviously in bad trouble. The whole area of his damaged foot was swollen and there were lumps and bumps sticking out of his stocking.

I signalled for a stretcher and had him taken to hospital. When the specialist told me there was no fracture I was surprised. In a way I wish there had been because it would have been cured within three or four months.

Frank had dislocated the joints of the forefoot, and close to the ankle joint. Frank, as much due to his own dedication, got over it, but it was a tricky one. Again, it doesn't make me a clever chap, but because of my training I was able to help his recovery, part of my training concerned this joint.

We know when it's right to give a pain-killing injection and when it

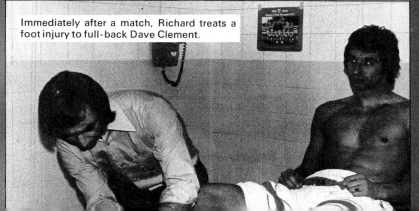

Immediately after a match, Richard treats a foot injury to full-back Dave Clement.

only serves to see a player through a game, at the same time doing further damage to his injury.

We do know, I can assure you, when a player is "acting" and when he is either down and still because he really needs attention. Even when a player goes down in mock injury for tactical reasons. Oh yes, some clubs do that, I can tell you. And I'm not being plain loyal when I say we won't tolerate that kind of thing at Rangers. For a start our players are much too sensible and disciplined. Yes, I have to admit players even over-react to tackles to try to get an opponent sent off.

But back to that pain-killing injection. There are times when it can kill more than the pain. It can put a

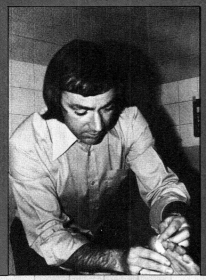

player out of action for a long time. We are trained to know when it's on, the "bucket and sponge man" is not.

I'd only agree to a "wrong" jab for something like a Cup Final, when, say, a goalkeeper has the summer to recover naturally with the help of nature.

OK, so we've thousands of pounds worth of electronic equipment to treat our stars. But what about those of you who play on the public parks, lucky to have even one St. John Ambulance man around?

There's no high frequency electro-magnetic currents you can switch on. No ultrasonic equipment. Just a guy who runs the team with a big heart.

If you have a friendly association with a local League club, you'd be surprised how much help you can get. But it's important to report your injury. Don't try to be the hero and play through it. You'll do more damage that way.

You see, pain after a game might mean nothing, but it *could* mean a cracked bone. Don't be frightened to ask for advice. Go to a hospital, and if you are attached as a schoolboy player to a professional club, ask to see the physiotherapist.

Don't forget before a game to do a warm-up, stretching your muscles. It's the best prevention of torn or pulled muscles I know.

Don't play with strappings on if you can help it. They are restrictive and can weaken your muscles.

Don't try to run off an injury if you are hurt in a game. Wait for your trainer to have a look at it first.

Now, I've no wish to join the

referee-bashing clan. I happen to believe they have a very difficult job and in the main do it very well. An injured player is just a drop in the ocean as far as their problems are concerned. They've got to keep the play moving. But as a medical man I feel they must let US on to determine the seriousness of an injury. Nine out of ten are not at all serious, but the tenth one just could be a fracture, or a serious wounds.

Some referees even try to pick up an injured player. That's wrong.

On one occasion Mick Leach had blood, lots of it, coming from a wound caused by studs. The referee rightly called me on immediately.

Others aren't so quick. I'm not a rebel, but I've been booked twice and sent off once.

The bookings were for misunderstanding a signal to go on to treat a player. The sending off? Well, it happened like this. We were playing Telstar, in Holland, on a pre-season tour. Dave Clement had been suffering from an ankle injury and he went down after a bad tackle. I ran on to treat him, the referee pointed to the bench, then walked across and pointed to the dressing-rooms. I had to sit out the last 25 minutes in the stand.

It's not all serious in professional football. I'm not going to tell you about some of the places I have been asked to put a piece of plaster on match days. But I can tell you about the young apprentice who came in to see me with an ankle injury.

Trying to find the most painful area I asked him where it hurt. The conversation went on like this. He said: "To the left, to the right, up a bit, down a bit." At that point I asked him if he thought we were playing the "Golden Shot".

Then there was the youngster who came in on Monday morning and said he thought he had pulled a hamstring. I asked him at what stage he was taken off on Saturday in the youth team game. "I didn't play," he replied.

So, when did you do it? I asked. "It was like this," he answered, "I went to a dance on Saturday night, and I was running for a bus when I felt it go."

That one went down in the medical book as "pulled hamstring, running for a bus."

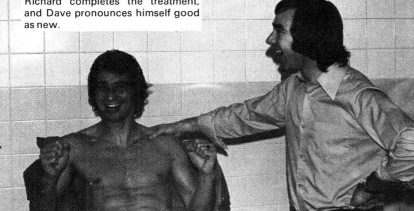

Richard completes the treatment, and Dave pronounces himself good as new.

Published by IPC Magazines Ltd., Kings Reach Tower, Stamford Street, London, S.E.1., England. Sole agents for Australia and New Zealand, Gordon & Gotch Ltd., South Africa: Central News Agency Ltd. Printed in England by Fleetway Printers, Gravesend, Kent. Cover laminated by Olro Coatings Ltd. using Bexphane film.

FRANCIS LEE
DERBY COUNTY